Presentations That Change Minds

STRATEGIES TO PERSUADE, CONVINCE, AND GET RESULTS

Josh Gordon

McGraw-Hill

New York | Chicago | San Francisco | Lisbon | London
Madrid | Mexico City | Milan | New Delhi
San Juan | Seoul | Singapore | Sydney | Toronto

The **McGraw·Hill** Companies

1 2 3 4 5 6 7 8 9 0   FGR/FGR   0 9 8 7 6 5

ISBN 0-07-146109-4

McGraw-Hill books are available at special quantity discounts to use as premiums and sales promotions, or for use in corporate training programs. For more information, please write to the Director of Special Sales, McGraw-Hill Professional, Two Penn Plaza, New York, NY 10121-2298. Or contact your local bookstore.

 This book is printed on recycled, acid-free paper containing a minimum of 50% recycled, de-inked fiber.

Library of Congress Cataloging-in Publication Data

Gordon, Josh.
  Presentations that change minds : strategies to persuade, convince, and get results / by Josh Gordon.
    p. cm.
  ISBN 0-07-146109-4 (alk. paper)
  1. Business presentations. 2. Public speaking. I. Title.
  HF5718.22.G67 2005

651.7'3—dc22   2005024656

For my wife, Lynn. After 19 years, you're still the love of my life.

Contents

Acknowledgments   vii

Introduction: How This Book Will Make You More Successful   ix

The Five Unbreakable Rules of Persuasive Presentations   xi

1. The Presentation That Deeply Involves Your Audience   1

2. The Presentation That Creates Excitement   17

3. The Presentation That Persuades with a Story   35

4. The Presentation That Sells a New Idea   53

5. The Presentation That Persuades by Emotional Appeal   69

6. The Presentation That Persuades with Humor   83

7. The Presentation That Lays Out "The Facts"   99

8. The Presentation That Inspires   119

9. The Presentation That Changes a Perception   137

10. The Presentation That Builds Trust   155

11. The Presentation That Offers a Solution   171

12. The Presentation That Makes a Financial Case   185

13. The Presentation That Gets Them to Choose You
over the Competition   203

14. The Presentation That Wins over a Hostile Audience   221

Appendix A: The "Eyes Rules"   237

Appendix B: Picking the Right Strategy, by the Numbers   241

Appendix C: Gender and Political Affiliation Contrast Study   253

Index   259

Acknowledgments

Many people worked behind the scenes to make this book possible in addition to those I've quoted throughout, and their efforts deserve special acknowledgment.

Thanks go to Dave Smith from the Walt Disney Company, Norma Saken from Lee Iacocca and Company, and the helpful researchers at the John Fitzgerald Kennedy Library, for their help during my researching of the stories introducing each chapter.

At McGraw-Hill, thanks go to my editor Donya Dickerson, and also to the editorial director Mary Glenn, with whom I am delighted to be working again after she supervised the editing of my book, *Tough Calls*, years ago.

Thanks to my daughters, Laura and Jenny, for sharing their dad's attention with this book for far too many evenings and weekends while it was being written. Thanks also to my wife, Lynn, who slogged her way through all of my "creative" spelling and wording to bring its quality and clarity up immeasurably.

The research could not have been done without the help of Joanne Melton, publisher of *Presentations* magazine and Gerhard Gschwandtner, publisher of *SellingPower* magazine, who generously helped with the deployment of my surveys.

A long overdue thanks to book agent extraordinaire, Daniel Greenberg, who broke me into the big time.

Thank you all.

Introduction

How This Book Will Make You More Successful

Presentations are the heavy artillery of persuasion. There are many tools of persuasion such as phone conversations, meetings, e-mail, and letters. But the approach reserved for the most critical persuasive encounters, with the most important customers, managers, peers, voters, or the many committees that can determine our fate, is the face-to-face presentation. The ability to persuade in this most important of all communication venues is the essential skill for success.

This book will give you an edge by helping you to become a more persuasive presenter. If you have been on the receiving end of other presentations designed to persuade, you may realize already that most of them fail. The problem is that presenters often don't realize just how diffcrent persuasive presentations are from any other kind of presentation. When persuasive presentations are created with the same template as those designed to inform or educate, few audience members will change their minds. This book breaks new ground by treating persuasive presentations as an entirely new species.

The result of research on the greatest persuasive presenters the world has ever seen, surveys involving thousands of respondents, and dozens of contemporary interviews, *Presentations That Change Minds* lays out cold the only 14 persuasive approaches you will ever need to dramatically increase your persuasive power. The power of each of these approaches is captured in each of the 14 chapters of this book. Each chapter will take you step by step as you plan, design, present, and close with a presentation that uses one particular approach. I have covered each one of them separately in this book because the construction of each type of presentation is unique unto itself. For example, to achieve maximum impact, a presentation that persuades by emotional appeal must be planned, visualized, created, and shared differently from a presentation that persuades by making a financial case. Of course, as you apply these approaches to your own particular challenges, you may want to blend some of them together. You may start your presentation with humor, for instance, and then go on to offer a solution.

Presentations That Change Minds gives you access to the power of these approaches like never before. Are you ready to become more successful by mastering the power of persuasive presentations?

Turn the page.

The Five Unbreakable Rules of Persuasive Presentations

Rule No. 1: A Persuasive Presentation Always Advocates a Competitive Option

If you are in product sales or running for political office, you know who or what your competition is. But if you are selling an idea or trying to get a budget approved, your competition may be less obvious. When seeking budget approval, your competition could be the possibility of having your budget approved at a lower dollar level, or other departments in your own company trying to siphon funds away from yours. If you are presenting a new idea, your competition could be a different idea or merely the status quo. In many cases, "not changing," or apathy, is your biggest competitor.

Typically, your audience may not think about your product or option as being in a constant state of competition, but as a presenter wanting to change how your audience thinks or feels, you have entered a competitive world. With every persuasive presentation there are products, options, or ideas, which, if accepted, will prevent your audience from accepting yours.

Rule No. 2: A Persuasive Presentation
Strengthens and Deepens Dialogue, Not Control

The least persuasive presentation starts on slide one and seeks total control to make the audience "hear every word and see every slide," right through to the end. Without recognition that your audience has a unique consciousness, dialogue shuts down.

In order to change an audience's collective heart and mind you need to constantly read that audience and adjust your presentation's pacing, tone, and content for maximum impact. As they react to what you say and do, you will get strong indicators of what they believe. For masters of the craft, presenting to an audience is a completely interactive process well before the questions and answers begin.

A persuasive presentation is a process in which an audience tries a new idea, product, or concept on for size. There is never a perfect fit right away. There is always a need for questions to be answered, concerns aired, more detail shared, and pricing and competitive information explained. Without dialogue there is little persuasion.

Rule No. 3: A Persuasive Presentation
Is a Persuasive Event, Not a Slide Show

As I begin to plan a persuasive presentation, I start by asking, "What can I *do* to change my audience's hearts and minds? What can I do to help them understand, motivate them to feel, show them contrast, get them excited, make them nervous or uncomfortable, help them to trust, get them involved, get them to laugh, or see a financial benefit, that will win acceptance for my product or option?

After I decide on what I need to do, I then start to think about how best to communicate or involve my audience. Very often I settle on the tried-and-true PowerPoint style presentation, but not always. On the following pages you will see examples of presentations that persuade through interactive exercises, stories, and humor.

Put your audience first. Start by thinking about what you need to do to persuade them, not what you want to put on your first slide.

Rule No. 4: A Persuasive Presentation Targets an Audience's Decision-Making Process

Unlike presentations that train, educate, or just inform, persuasive presentations seek to change how an audience thinks or feels. But this change must begin with an understanding of how they make decisions. I once was successful in persuading an audience that I had the highest-quality product possible to buy, but I made no sale. I later discovered that my audience did not want the "highest-quality" product but instead one that was "good enough" and cheapest. I did a great job of presenting my product but a lousy job targeting my audience's decision-making process.

A persuasive presentation must be strategically planned and delivered so that if you change an audience's mind or feeling they will be moved to action in the way you want. Without sensitivity to the decision-making process, your goals will not be realized.

Rule No. 5: A Persuasive Presentation Asks for an Order

A persuasive presentation has a goal. Before you leave your audience, you either want to achieve that goal or understand what the next step toward achieving it will be.

An audience is a decision driver. If all the decision makers are in the audience, you have a unique opportunity to gain agreement to proceed on the spot. If the decision makers are elsewhere, a presentation can become an event whereby a product or option gains acceptance and can move to the next level.

In a sales presentation, if you don't ask for the order you won't get it. The same is true of all persuasive presentations.

The Presentation That Deeply Involves Your Audience

Tell me and I forget, teach me and I may remember, involve me and I learn.—Benjamin Frankin (1706–1790)

You must get involved to have an impact. No one is impressed with the won-lost record of the referee.—Napoleon Hill (1883–1970)

In motivating people, you've got to engage their minds and their hearts. I motivate people, I hope, by example—and perhaps by excitement, by having productive ideas to make others feel involved.—Rupert Murdoch (Chairman & Chief Executive, News Corporation; 1931–)

You find out who your real friends are when you're involved with a scandal.—Elizabeth Taylor (Actress; 1932–)

Just after World War II, Walter Elias Disney had a hard time getting support and involvement from people who could fund his idea for a new kind of amusement park. Even at his own company, The Walt Disney Company, his brother Roy, who ran the studio's finances, refused to provide money for development studies, fearing a stockholder rebellion if he supported such a risky proposition. Walt funded the first development studies himself by selling his vacation property and borrowing against his personal life insurance.

But the studies offered no good news to motivate investors. Consultant Harrison "Buzz" Price recalls: "The highlight of our feasibility analysis took place at the Amusement Park Annual Convention and Trade Show in November 1953.... We cornered four of the nation's leading amusement park owners and fed them Chivas Regal and caviar in our suite. We presented the concept of the park in a two-hour evening session. The reaction was unanimous. It would not work.... 'Mr. Disney's park idea is too expensive to build and too expensive to operate. Tell your boss to save his money.'"

Skepticism continued as Disney approached amusement industry ride and equipment suppliers for products to support his concept. Richard Schickel wrote in *The Disney Version*: "Early in 1954, Disney sent four staffers off on an around-the-country tour looking for ideas at established amusement parks and the firms that manufactured equipment for them. The only idea on which they found general agreement was that Disney was crazy."

With no involvement from banks, Disney turned to the television networks for funding. In 1954 television was in its infancy, and Hollywood studios, fearing a new competitor, had steered clear of producing shows for the medium. Disney's offer to become the first Hollywood studio to produce a weekly TV show carried a lot of appeal as well as a catch: the network that broadcast it had to help fund his theme park. Roy Disney, now on board for the project, packed off to New York City with a large fold-out illustration of the Disneyland theme park to present the Disneyland concept to the three television networks. After NBC and CBS turned Roy Disney down, he found a backer in ABC, which was then in last place among the networks and desperate for a hit show.

"The Disneyland Story," the first show on the *Disneyland* program (as the Disney show was then called), aired on October 27, 1954, and was hosted by Walt Disney himself. Disney, wooden pointer in hand, presented the Disneyland concept: how the TV show and the park were related, what the different "lands" of Disneyland were, and what kind of entertainment could be expected from each. During his presentation, Disney made reference to a large, wall-mounted illustration of the theme park, which looked very much like the one Roy had used in his presentations in New York City.

The first TV show was a monster hit that immediately involved the American public. According to *Time* magazine, it was "a bang that blew Wednesday night to kingdom come for the [other] two major networks." Disney's personal presentation of the Disneyland concept that began the program generated a huge positive reaction; it paved the way for a hugely successful opening day when Disneyland opened about a year later.

Audience involvement is a delicate thing. Disney's presentation on ABC gained instant involvement for a national audience eager to learn more about Disneyland and the possibility of a visit. But the same man, presenting the same concept with similar presentation materials, obtained little audience involvement from unreceptive bankers, amusement park operators, and amusement park equipment suppliers. But through it all, Disney was confident he could involve his ultimate audience: the national TV viewers willing to visit Disneyland.

HOW THIS WORKS

If your audience is involved with what you present, they will be persuaded by it. Without involvement there is no audience persuasion.

Pitfalls

Thinking That If You Have an Audience's Attention You Have Their Involvement

It is possible to hold an audience's attention with entertaining stories and jokes and yet have no audience involvement. Entertainment does not always mean persuasion. Audience involvement means your audience is actively comparing what you are sharing with what they already know, evaluating it, raising concerns, and participating in a dialogue. There are always concerns and objections that need addressing in the persuasion process.

Step by Step: Preparation

Great presenters can make audience involvement look effortless. But often there is a lot of preparation and planning that goes on beforehand. The following are some approaches to consider.

Involvement through Relevancy

According to Jim Endicott, president of Distinction Communication, Inc. (www.Distinction-services.com), "Probably the greatest mistake presenters make is to take the traditional approach:

here's who we are, here's what we do, here's our product, do you have questions?" Endicott says that this approach is very common but creates zero relevance to the issues that your audience is facing. Endicott advocates talking about the difficulties your audience is experiencing first, not your company or product.

Brad Gleeson, president and COO of Active Light, a company that facilitates digital signage networks and visual systems, tries to put himself in the mind of an audience member before he gives a presentation. Gleeson might ask himself, "If I were a system integrator, or if I were a retailer, what might I expect and what information might I be looking for?" Then he looks for relevant information to present.

David Scelba, CEO of SG&W Integrated Marketing Communications, once had to give a presentation before a group of thoracic surgeons. These heart surgeons save peoples' lives every day, and he feared that this group could be among the most intimidating, hard-to-involve audiences ever. But, Scelba had a plan.

He began by referencing the open-heart surgery that had recently been done on former President Bill Clinton. Initially, Clinton's surgeons had considered performing his operation with newer, "closed chest" techniques, but eventually they opted for the open-heart approach. The surgeons in the room had strong opinions about this high-profile case, and Scelba had a highly animated dialogue within seconds of bringing the subject up.

Involvement through Fun

Evilee Thibeault, CEO and publisher of *Network World, Inc.*, was once facing a presentation "cattle call." Before this particular buying committee would see her presentation, they would already have seen many others. With a tight time limit for her presentation, her challenge was to get immediate involvement from this worn-out committee.

As soon as the committee entered Thibeault's presentation room, they were completely taken by surprise. The lights were turned down and music from a boom box was blasting "The Money Song." Committee members were given an enthusiastic welcome, leis were placed around their necks, and they were invited to dance along with Thibeault's team, who was already up dancing to the music.

When the room settled down, Thibeault's group blasted "The Money Song" one more time, saw to it that chocolate coins were shared all around, and then announced, "This presentation is about the money and how we can help your client make more of it!" The weary committee greeted the start of the presentation with enthusiastic applause.

Involvement through Emotion

David Scelba says the way to get an audience emotionally involved is to first find some kind of common ground, often outside of the content of the presentation itself: "Say, you are presenting and you realize most of the people in the room are young parents. Then find a way to make your point as it relates to kids. If you have kids yourself, mention your own kids… and you have established common ground that they can relate to."

Sometimes you have to read the audience to find this kind of common ground, but Scelba insists that if you take the time to look for it, you will always find something you share in common.

Once the audience sees commonality in you, they might consider accepting your emotions as their own. But Scelba insists the job is not yet done: "A lot of presenters are afraid to express themselves in an emotional way. If you are passionate about what you are delivering, you need to show them with emotion in your voice, hand and body motions." If you can establish commonality and express your emotions strongly, your audience will become emotionally involved in your presentation.

Involvement through Problem Solving

My wife, Lynn, is a smart shopper who has no patience for salespeople who waste her time. As we entered a store in New York City's lighting district, we spotted a lighting fixture that looked like the one we had been considering buying for our living room. When Lynn asked the salesperson if it was indeed that particular model, the salesperson said it was not, and scooted off to check her catalogues. Meanwhile, Lynn flipped over the price tag on the unit to reveal that the fixture was in fact the one we wanted. My wife shook her head as we headed for the door, "How can she help us if she doesn't even know what's in her own showroom?"

The next store had another fixture that we might also have considered. But as I took out a camera to take a picture for comparison, a shop manager scolded, "Hey, no pictures in here!" My wife frowned at the unfriendly act and said, "That's OK, we were just leaving."

Another store had the unit but when we asked the staffer what metal finish would look best in our 1860 brownstone he said sloppily, "Hey, if you really want my opinion, they all look great." Lynn whispered to me, "Next!"

"Next" was Herb, a salesperson more senior than the others and at first, less friendly. However, unlike the others, he took the time to find out how he could help us. He said slowly, "So... you've got a brownstone that needs lighting." He asked questions about our furniture, layout, and personal tastes, and then offered lots of helpful advice and information. We not only bought the original fixture we came in for but lighting for the entire floor. Herb understood that we needed someone who could immediately get involved in our problem and help us solve it. We were not looking to invest in a relationship just because someone was acting friendly. Believe me, without Herb's good advice and useful information, Lynn would have headed for the door.

Involvement through Activities

When attempting to emphasize the importance of limiting the number of topics you throw at an audience during a presentation, Jim Endicott throws a beach ball at his audience. He explains, "Of course, whenever a beach ball goes into an audience, people hit it back and forth. I tell them, 'It's not that tough to keep one beach ball in play. It's fun.'" With that, Endicott throws in a second ball. "This is like introducing a second concept into your presentation. This is still manageable, isn't it?" Then Endicott launches four or five more beach balls into the audience and chaos results. This makes Endicott's point. In addition, the audience has physically interacted in a fun way and will be more likely to interact in other ways as well. Afterwards their defenses are down and they will be more likely to become involved.

Involvement through Graphics and Charts

When planning your charts and graphics, you can use them as an involvement starter, not just for factual support.

Pat Wiesner, retired CEO of Weisner Publishing, shares: "I don't like presentations where people read to me off the chart. I think that's almost insulting. What you need to do is write your slide in such a way that it's a lifting-off point for what you have to say."

Charts that show relationships or contrast between features, competitors, or issues are great involvement starters. Think about designing slides so that when you show them you can stand back and ask your audience, "Is this how you see it?" Or, "do you agree with what this slide shows?" Concludes Wiesner, "If you are just going to read me a 20-chart presentation, just send me the thing, and I'll read it myself."

Involvement through Ego

While Ted O'Brien, who was for many years the narrator of PBS's *Nova* series, was asked to narrate a public service announcement, four executives from the ad agency handed Ted the copy for the 30-second spot.

Ted, no stranger to this type of work, read the copy through the way he normally would for these kinds of spots. Three of the executives loved it, but the fourth wanted just a little change. The concerned executive thought Ted's second take was great, as did two of the others, but the last guy said, "You know, if you could just make one slight change…" In the next few minutes each executive had something to say about a slightly different read.

"The fifth take," Ted recalls, "was exactly like the first take, but this time they all loved it. I walked away thinking, you know what that was? They were thinking, 'if I don't have something to say about this, who needs me?'"

Many audiences will initially jump in and become involved just because they need to get their two cents in. When presenting to an audience, think about what kind of expertise will be present in that room. Often if you ask an open-ended question where audience members can reveal their knowledge of the subject, you can get immediate involvement. Ask, "What do you think about the new industry regulations passed last week?" Or, "What does anyone know about _____?"

Involvement through Spontaneity

David Ross, president of Ross Video, recalls a time when he was talked into doing an hourly, live stage presentation at his trade show booth during a major exhibition.

Ross and a co-presenter were on stage while their script called for back-and-forth banter to reveal product details. The presentation fell flat the first time out.

He explains, "To the horror of the person that was working with me, I said, 'Just work with me. Throw the script away.'" Ross started saying things to get reactions, whatever came to mind. Ross recalls: "Suddenly we were drawing crowds every hour because we were having so much fun together. I realized, this is the way to get people engaged. This was a live perform-ance and no two were alike."

Live presentations drew audience involvement because no one was sure what was going to happen next.

Involvement through Relevant Entertainment

Jeff Reinhardt, senior vice president at Primedia Business, draws involvement by building magic tricks into his presentations. Reinhardt says, "I find that using magic creates a fun meeting, a connection with my audience, and makes my points memorable."

In a presentation where Reinhardt was talking about the chal-lenges of partnering with competitors, he used a magic trick called "magic mentalism" to create the illusion that he was read-ing someone's mind. The trick dramatized the point that when you do consider partnering with a competitor for mutual gain, it is extremely important to understand what they are really expecting or thinking—if only you could read their mind. But of course you can't read people's minds, which is why communication is so important. The magic trick drew in even the most disinterested members of Reinhardt's audience.

Involvement by Room Setup

If you have the power to set up the room where you give a presentation, you have the power to set the stage for a positive reception. The following are a couple of ways to encourage or discourage involvement through room setup:

Encourages Involvement	Discourages Involvement
Chairs in a circle or semi-circle	Chairs arranged in auditorium style
Presenter on audience's level	Presenter at podium

Step by Step: The Presentation

Be an Audience Detective

Audiences do not overtly tell you what they are thinking. As you stand up in front of them, you often have to be an audience detective to find out what you need to know.

For great presenters, this all happens intuitively in the blink of an eye. Let's take a slow-motion look at the first two minutes of a presentation. The first few sentences a presenter shares are like feelers that reach out to tickle, provoke, stimulate, or touch every audience member. Some sentences will carry more impact than others, but each will have weight, a dimension, and will elicit some kind of response or feedback.

The presenter then takes notice of these reactions. As the audience settles in and focuses on the presenter's message, the presenter will notice subtle shifts in the mood of the room, the body language of the audience, and facial expressions.

As the presentation continues, the well-practiced presenter knows typical reactions to certain parts of her presentation. The passage she now comes to typically causes an audience to smile. This audience did not. What does that mean? Another passage typically holds an audience in suspense for a minute or so. This audience is not following suit. The presenter adjusts accordingly. She may slow down certain passages, speed up others, skip sections, become more emotional, or add an extra story. These adjustments happen on an intuitive level, often without the presenter even thinking about them.

The presenter now starts to anticipate the kinds of reactions she can expect and makes further adjustments. Even before the question-and-answer section, a presentation can be a completely interactive process. As the presentation proceeds, one millisecond at a time, this constant evaluation and recalibration of message will create a vastly different result than if the content is just transferred from point A to point B.

Great presenters see themselves, not as gatekeepers through which content flows, but as lightening rods for feedback, content modifiers, and, above all else, real-time managers of a dynamic communication process.

Monitor and Pace for Different Levels of Sophistication

In 1997 I was giving a presentation on my new book *Tough Calls: Selling Strategies to Win Over Your Most Difficult Customers* at a local bookstore. The book signing became a family affair as my wife and then-six-year-old daughter Laura came along with some neighbors.

With slides projecting on the bookstore wall, I took 15 minutes to talk about the three worst problem clients I covered in my book: the client who grinds you on price, the client who is indifferent, and the client who complains about everything. When my presentation was complete I asked for questions. In her most businesslike tone, my six-year-old asked brightly, "Daddy, I have one question... what's a client?" Clearly, I had missed the mark for at least one member of my audience.

As you present, it is important to realize the people in your audience will have varying levels of sophistication. To be effective, you need to address all levels.

The Iacocca Effect

It has been said that when Bill Clinton, Ronald Reagan, or Lee Iacocca talks to an audience, whether it be five people, or five million, every member of that audience feels as if he is talking to him alone.

I saw this firsthand when I interviewed Lee Iacocca while writing my previous book, *Selling 2.0: Motivating Customers in the New Economy.* I interviewed over 100 of the top sales managers in the world's leading corporations and asked them a simple question: "How do you motivate your customers to buy?"

In all but two of my interviews, the response to this question was a description of my interviewee's selling approaches, accomplishments, and success stories. But my interview with Iacocca was different. Instead of jumping right in and responding to my question, he asked one of his own. He politely said, "Wait a minute. Hold on, Josh, what is this book about anyway?" After

I explained the book, Iacocca had a few more questions. I had prepared to ask him all the questions and was surprised to be answering so many myself. When Iacocca heard that I lived in Brooklyn, he shared that some of his fondest childhood memories came from times spent just a few miles from where I live. Iacocca had shifted the point of view of our dialogue to my perspective; the book I was writing, my town of Brooklyn. "Now, did you have some questions you wanted to ask me?" he finally asked. I sure did, but it did not feel like I was interviewing a corporate giant. It felt like I was just having a casual conversation with one of my Brooklyn neighbors.

Clinton, Reagan, and Iacocca all are confident but not boastful, show a sincere interest in their audience, and, most importantly, present through the point of view of their audience. Just like Mr. Iacocca did with me that day.

Closing

Audience involvement results in commitment. This is not about sales technique, it is simply human nature. A great illustration of how this works comes from a book written in 1889 called *The Art of Selling*. In it, author F. B. Goddard describes how one salesman wins over a merchant's order that the previous salesman failed to get by winning the merchant's involvement:

> One [salesperson] introduces himself as the representative of a house; his address is respectful and pleasant, and the merchant glances over his samples, and listens to his arguments respecting styles, qualities and prices, put forward in the usual manner, from the manifest standpoint of self-interest and desire to effect a sale.

At length the merchant says, "I am glad to make your acquaintance, but trade is dull and collections slow, and I don't feel like buying today. I will keep your card, however, and when you are in town again, touch in and we may give you an order...." The next day, perhaps, another salesman calls with similar goods and prices. But, somehow, he gets nearer to the merchant. His talk is quite sensible, not stereotyped, and it interests him. He seems to enter into the practice spirit of the merchant's business, to realize his hopes and his struggles, and to appreciate his prudence. He touches upon details, and every day results clearly stand out. He makes it plain that goods must be bought, or they cannot be sold; yet he does not try to sell him more than he thinks it prudent for him to buy. In short, his suggestions and recommendations are characterized by an intelligent interest in the welfare of the man he is dealing with; he aims to do as he would be done by, and he shows it. The result is, he goes away with an order, and leaves behind him a customer and a friend. In such things lies the difference between the salesmen, both in the wholesale and retail trade.

Greater involvement leads to better dialogue, which leads to better understanding, which leads to an acceptance of what you are proposing. If your audience is involved in what you are saying, and if you sense they are headed for accepting a commitment, ask: "We have had some good back and forth on this proposal. Would you consider moving forward on this?"

2

The Presentation That Creates Excitement

A mediocre idea that generates enthusiasm will go further than a great idea that inspires no one.—Mary Kay Ash (founder of Mary Kay Cosmetics; 1915–2001)

New habits can be launched ... on condition of there being new stimuli and new excitements.—William James (philosopher and psychologist, leader of the philosophical movement of Pragmatism; 1842–1910)

Every great and commanding movement in the annals of the world is due to the triumph of enthusiasm. Nothing great was ever achieved without it.—Ralph Waldo Emerson (philosopher, poet, essayist; 1803–1882)

In 1974, the real estate scene in midtown New York City was grim. The famous Chrysler Building was in foreclosure; and just across the street, the Commodore Hotel had a sleazy flea market operating on the ground floor alongside boarded-up storefronts where derelicts would spend the night. It was a depressing sight.

But as 27-year-old Donald Trump approached the Commodore Hotel, he saw something different. Trump recalls in his autobiography: "It was about 9 in the morning. And there were thousands of well-dressed Connecticut and Westchester commuters flooding onto the street from Grand Central Terminal and the subway below. The city was on the verge of bankruptcy, but what I saw was a superb location."

Knowing that the hotel was up for sale, Trump thought what was needed was a fundamentally new way to look at this location. Trump's vision was not just to renovate the hotel back from the point of decay but also to come up with a dazzling new design that recast it into a showcase for luxury. He met with a young, enthusiastic architect named Der Scutt and challenged him with the project. Trump instructed Scutt to make his drawings look like they had spent a huge sum of money on them. After all, recalled Trump, "a good-looking presentation goes a long way."

Using Scutt's drawings to sell the sizzle, Trump persuaded the Hyatt Corporation to partner with him on the project. On May 4, 1975, Trump and Hyatt called a joint press conference, announcing their agreement as partners to purchase and transform the Commodore Hotel—assuming they could get financing.

But obtaining financing in a city on the verge of bankruptcy proved a huge challenge. As bank after bank turned Trump down, his own father described his son's efforts to buy the hotel as "fighting for a seat on the Titanic."

Trump was certain that if he could get a tax abatement from the New York Board of Estimate a bank would lend him money.

Two weeks before the board was scheduled to meet, a competing offer to renovate the Commodore surfaced from another developer. This proposal would keep the Commodore largely intact with minimal investment. This less ambitious plan asked the board for far less tax relief and concessions than Trump's proposal.

In the end, though, it was the sizzle and excitement of Trump's vision that swayed the board. On May 20, 1976, the Board of Estimate voted unanimously to give Trump the tax abatement he needed to get his bank loans.

Today, few guests enjoying the luxury accommodations at New York's Grand Hyatt Hotel know that they owe their comfort, in part, to a presentation that sparked excitement at a time in New York City history when few saw more than gloom.

HOW THIS WORKS

When an audience gets truly excited about what you are presenting they are easily moved to action.

Pitfalls

Thinking You Create Excitement by Immediately Hitting Your Audience with "Everything You've Got"

The presentation that generates excitement is a building process. You must incrementally take an audience to ever-greater levels of enthusiasm.

When I began researching the speeches of Dr. Martin Luther King, Jr., I, like most people, had already seen the film clips of the dramatic conclusions to his "I Have a Dream" and "I've Been to the Mountaintop" speeches. I was surprised to find then, when I listened to recordings of these speeches from their beginning, that they actually started at a snail's pace.

King, who to the very end described himself as "fundamentally a clergyman, a Baptist preacher," followed the Baptist "calm to storm" formula for sermon delivery. The first few lines of most of his presentations were delivered in an exaggeratedly slow, unemotional monotone, often with several-second-long pauses between sentences. As his speech rolled on, he would pick up speed and emotion until excitement crackled through the air at its conclusion.

Thinking That Excitement Starts with Your Product or Option

There is a parable about the advice that the world's greatest drill bit salesperson gave to the new hire on the sales staff. The newcomer had spent the nights and weekends of his first six months on the job memorizing every detail of drill bit technology and every detail of the company's product line, yet the old pro continually sold circles around the newcomer and generated far more excitement wherever he went. As the newcomer pleaded with the old pro to share his secret, the pro said simply, "I don't know nearly as much as you do about the technology of drill bits, but I know far more about putting a ¼-inch hole in a piece of wood."

Audiences rarely get truly excited about products, services, or ideas that are offered to them in presentations. They do get truly excited about how products, services, or ideas effect or benefit them. Excitement starts with the needs, passions, hopes, and desires of your audience, not the specifics of your product or option.

Thinking Your Audience Will Automatically Be Enthusiastic If You Are

It cannot be emphasized enough how important your own personal enthusiasm is in creating excitement. But how you use your enthusiasm should reflect the unique needs of your audience. If you are presenting to a very skeptical audience, a big dose of enthusiasm early on can be viewed as "technique" and turn people off. Your enthusiasm is where a presentation that creates excitement begins. But it is just the first step, not the whole process.

Step by Step: Preparation

Start by Finding Your Audience's Passions

As I started a master's degree program in educational media to further my media production career, I was dismayed to discover that part of my requirement was a class in library science. Being a creative type with media production ambitions, I was not a likely candidate for success. My library science professor regarded me as a nonbeliever who had wandered into her flock by mistake. She called on me when I seemed confused or bored, which was often, and I thought she secretly wanted to flunk me.

By year's end I was close to failing library science; my only salvation lay in a year-end paper that would determine a large part of my grade. Desperate to avoid failing, I approached my professor and, reminding her that my degree would be in Educational Media, asked if I could produce a media program on library science to satisfy this requirement. She agreed.

As I began my research, I was surprised to find the details of library science even more boring than I had anticipated. To counter this I took a broad-stroke, dramatic look at the subject, casting library science far beyond just libraries, to being the historical guardians of civilization's knowledge. Using a well-constructed script, marvelous historical pictures, and a well-mixed dramatic sound track, a slide show emerged that presented library science as a dynamic force in the development of civilization itself. On the day our papers were due, the lights dimmed and my slide show hit the screen. It went smoothly enough, but as the lights came on, I was surprised to see tears streaming down my professor's cheeks. A startled student sitting to her side asked, "Professor, are you crying?" She wiped the tears from her eyes and said, "I'm sorry. It was just so exciting."

I passed her class with a C+. The best lesson I learned from library science is that audiences can have deep passions for subjects they are truly excited about and that you might not realize this until you are standing in front of them. However, if you can find out what these passions are *before* you stand in front of them, you can always get them excited. As you start to plan your next presentation, ask or find out what really gets them excited.

Engineer "Kickers"

"Kickers" are theatrical or content surprises that can push your audience to the next level of excitement. The following are some examples.

When Steven Jobs introduced the Macintosh in 1984, his carefully orchestrated presentation included a "kicker" toward the end of his presentation. He began on stage by calmly reading the first verse of the Bob Dylan song, "The Times They Are a-Changing." This low-key beginning was followed by a fast-paced multimedia show with music from the movie soundtrack *Flashdance* rewritten with Apple lyrics. Then it was back to low key as then-CEO John Scully presented the company financials.

Then it was Jobs, the evangelist, who walked onstage with an unidentified case and placed it on a table. He began by recounting the history of the computer industry with Apple as the David battling for business against much larger computer Goliaths. His passion so fired up the audience that when he finally lifted a computer out of his mystery case and the name Macintosh glided across a large screen behind him, the crowd erupted into an enthusiastic standing ovation that continued for several minutes.

But Jobs still had a kicker.

As the applause died down, he commented that he had done enough talking and now it was time to let the Mac talk for itself. To the total surprise of the audience, the Macintosh, using a prototype voice synthesis program said, "Hello, I am Macintosh. It sure is great to get out of that bag. Unaccustomed as I am to public speaking, I'd like to share with you a maxim I thought of the first time I met an IBM mainframe: 'Never trust a computer you can't lift.'"

Again, the auditorium thundered with applause. Jobs followed with evangelical fervor that led the audience to delirium.

Engineering a voice-synthesized speech on a personal computer was quite a feat back in 1984. But no matter what surprises you are trying to engineer for your presentation, it will need to be planned. Surprises add a sense of excitement to any presentation. The key is to find surprises that motivate your audience.

Pete May, vice president at Primedia Business, was presenting to a French Canadian company with a co-worker who was also fluent in French. Pete knew that every member of this audience spoke French as their primary language. They started their presentation in English but at a prearranged point, when their presentation was seeking more involvement, slipped into French. Said May, "It really woke 'em up."

Norwood Smith, vice president of sales at the Tampa Bay Convention and Visitors Bureau, surprised an audience while giving a presentation by whipping out a pirate hat, placing it on his head, and introducing himself as Jose Gaspar, the notorious Spanish pirate who prowled the waters near Tampa Bay, Florida, until 1821. Says Smith, "At first they were quite surprised, then they caught on that, obviously, I'm not Gaspar. But it's fun to start from the character perspective. I can talk about the history of my destination and describe something unique about it."

As the New Boston Convention Center opened, Executive Director of the Boston Convention Marketing Center Milt Herbert engineered a surprise for a group of convention planners. First, a full motorcycle escort accompanied their bus ride from their hotel to the convention center. Both bus and escort made a full 360-degree loop around the convention center. Then, suddenly the huge doors of the facility opened and the bus drove right though the doorway and onto the convention center floor. The trip took only a few minutes, but the convention planners arrived dazzled and ready to hear more about the Boston Convention Center.

Pace for Impact

Question: What do the Academy Awards, a roller coaster ride, and your next presentation designed to generate excitement all have in common?

Answer: The same pacing.

Audiences remember excitement-based presentations from their high, or most exciting, point backwards. If the high point is really high, it colors recollections of the whole presentation. After you get off a thrilling roller coaster ride you are not think-ing about the slow parts. As you plan a presentation designed to create excitement, keep in mind that you needn't have enough surprises and thrills to keep the audience dazzled the entire time. This is fine because you'll want to use the slower sections to share important content. Slower sections also provide contrast to make the high points seem higher. The pattern found in almost every excitement-based presentation is the same. Let's try this theory out on the 2005 Academy Awards presentation as well as a typical roller coaster ride:

The 2005 Academy Awards started off with a bang as, early on, Hilary Swank won the Oscar for best actress in *Million Dollar Baby*. This was one of the biggest awards of the evening, but not *the* biggest. Likewise, your last roller coaster ride started off with a big drop, but not the biggest one of the ride.

Then excitement at the Academy Awards dropped to a lower level as some of the smaller awards were presented. If you weren't out fixing yourself a sandwich, this is where you could have heard the producer of the best short live action film, *Wasp*, exclaim, "this is the dog's bollocks" over her Oscar win. Your roller coaster ride goes into a slower series of dips.

Then, as Oscar night advanced to its exciting conclusion, a series of ever-more-significant awards were given until the evening concluded with a bang as the most highly anticipated award for Best Picture was presented. Your roller coaster ride follows the same pattern, with a series of ever-greater drops, with the biggest loop or drop being saved for last. Most of the time you will achieve the biggest impact by using this same pattern to organize your presentation.

Start by taking a hard look at all the sections of your presentation and evaluating how much excitement each will generate. Kickers or other surprises are in your presentation only to generate excitement. There may be content-heavy sections that are essential but not as exciting. Being sensitive to content requirements, follow the pattern above: Give them a big taste of excitement right away at the beginning, drop back to offer contrast and suspense, and then begin the slow and steady climb to give the biggest bang at the end.

Plant Early Converts

During Steven Jobs's Macintosh introduction in 1984, the front three rows of the auditorium were packed with the software engineers and designers who had just spent 20-hour days bringing the Macintosh to life. The meeting was actually Apple's annual shareholders meeting, not a typical place to find the tech people behind a new product in great numbers. But Jobs knew that these were true believers whom he could count on to help lead an enthusiastic charge.

If I know some of the people in an audience to whom I will be presenting, I call them before I get to the meeting to get them excited about my presentation. I know that having a few individuals in the audience who are presold can help move a group along the road to excitement more quickly.

Step by Step: Giving the Presentation
The Introduction

Share Enthusiasm by Telling Them Why. Building excitement with an audience must begin with your own enthusiasm. If you can't start out enthusiastic about what you are sharing, skip this chapter and try another approach.

Cameron Bishop, president and CEO of Ascend Media, says: "You can have all the facts and details in the world but if you can't package and present it with passion and conviction, you are not going to get the job done. In my world, if you have anything short of a total commitment and belief in what you are saying, people will see right through it."

One of the best ways to start off is to tell your audience why you are so excited. As you plan for your presentation, imagine you are standing in front of your audience and finish the following sentence:

I am excited to be sharing this presentation because:

_____

If you can craft a single sentence that articulates why you are excited it can go a long way toward rallying your supporters as well as converting the skeptics in the back row.

The Main Body

Knock Out the Logical. Excitement is emotional, not logical. But before you go for the higher goal of group excitement you have to make sure you have covered the logical basis for your argument. Enthusiasm building is a process of building momentum. You do not want to be halfway into that process and be brought down by an objection that could have easily been countered earlier on. I do this by sharing an assumption that my audience is at least sold on the basics. I ask,

"Is it safe to assume we all believe that ..."

"By now we all share the same feeling that ..."

If someone feels strongly and objects right then and there, fine. This is an appropriate part of the persuasion process. I just want to get it out of the way before I start to rally my audience.

Rally the Enthused. Not every audience member is going to get enthusiastic about what you are sharing at the same rate. I find that if I look around the room and focus more on the individuals who get excited first, it helps get them more excited and keeps my own enthusiasm moving forward as well. If you can get part of your audience more excited they will bring the rest of the group along. An audience, by its very nature, is a natural breeding ground for shared group feelings. Or, as Henry Wadsworth Longfellow said, "Enthusiasm begets enthusiasm."

Listen for the Hidden Powder Kegs. I was giving a presentation on "being more persuasive" to the sales staff of McDermott Printing Solutions when a hand was raised toward the back of the room. David Frank Rosenberg, director of strategic accounts and distribution, wanted to know how the sales staff could make these persuasive approaches work when many higher-level managers involved in the buying decisions would not even meet with them. Sensing urgency in the question, I asked if this was a challenge faced by the rest of my audience. They strongly concurred and, on the spot, I scrapped the rest of my prepared presentation and plunged into the new subject. You could just feel the energy in the room double; suddenly there was a real sense of excitement.

Often you can't just change the content of a presentation but you can change the tone, appeal, or pace. You can add stories, an example, or an analogy that makes the excitement connection. The illusion is that all the excitement comes from the presenter. But presenters who know how to generate excitement often do so by finding ways to discover and channel their audience's existing hopes, dreams, and passions.

Engineer Connections to Your Audience's Passions. Typically when a convention planning committee arrives to scout a convention center, says Milt Herbert, executive director of the Boston Convention Marketing Center, they are given a tour of the facility and asked a few questions about their event. But when the committee from Cisco Systems arrived, they received very different treatment.

Their visit started in a conference room where Herbert introduced the committee to his staff. He intentionally avoided the building tour—at least in the beginning. Instead he began by saying: "Tell me about your event. Tell me why it exists and what you're trying to accomplish." He also asked if their famous chairman, John Chambers, was going to speak and, if so, in what capacity.

Then, recalls Herbert, he took out a list of event details such as technology requirements and food requirements and started asking about them one after another, "like a machine gun." The Cisco people did most of the talking and they loved it. Herbert recalls that the committee enthusiastically talked about their event. It's not often they are so intensely asked about the details of the event that is so important to them.

Then Herbert was ready for that building tour. But he didn't just show them walls and floor space, he showed them their event as it would play out at the Boston Convention Center, room by room. As they arrived in the food preparation area he described how their food requirements that surfaced during his meeting would be met. Says Herbert, "The most important thing is that I tied my presentation back to the things they talked about in our meeting so I was feeding back to them their own event, using my building as the platform for how their event would work."

An independent convention planner who was a member of the Cisco delegation told Herbert his presentation was "the best presentation that any facility had ever given them." Cisco enthusiastically signed up for an event in Boston.

But Herbert refuses to take personal credit for their enthusiasm. Instead, he credits the hard work and attention to detail that made it possible to show the delegation an opportunity to make their event, which they were already excited about, even more exciting.

"It's not about me personally," he says. "It's great that they are excited about my facility, but if you asked them to describe me after the presentation, they might say, 'He's a tall guy, glasses, slightly thin.' That's it."

In any presentation that generates excitement, you need to tap into your audience's passions. There's no planting, inventing, or manipulating them. Your audience's passions already exist as they enter the room. Your job is to discover and connect to them, either because you have planned to do so or because you have discovered opportunities during the presentation itself.

Drive It to the Next Level. Here is the final challenge. As you stand in front of your audience near the end of your presentation, with whatever planned kickers or surprises you have not used, with whatever audience passions you have uncovered, with whatever opportunities you can now envision together, with whatever ideas you feel you can now share, with all of the personal passion you muster, you have to find a way to take the excitement in the room to the next level.

There is no logical step-by-step procedure for how you do this because it is different for every audience and presentation. But somehow, you must find something to say, ask, challenge, show, propose, or share that moves your audience from "extremely interested" to "very excited." If you do the right thing, something "clicks," and the room will fill with excitement and feel very different.

I find that if I have prepared well, listened deeply, and maintained my passion, something always occurs to me as to how this can be done. Often I have preplanned that "something" that makes the "click" and my job is just to find the right time to share it so my audience is really ready to hear or see it. Just as often it can be something spontaneous that develops from the presentation process.

Here are some "clicks" I have used:

→ With an audience struggling to understand the impact of a new technology, I "clicked" by showing my prepared Power-Point presentation on the subject, but I slowed down and added an on-the-spot customized tutorial that helped them understand the technology for the first time.

→ In another example audience members from a marketing department once shared that a competitor was outmaneuvering them. I shifted my discussion from "why they should buy magazine ad space from me" to ideas to counter their new threat (that eventually resulted in their buying ad space from me), and we clicked to the next level.

→ With an audience that I discovered was following the leadership principles of business consultant and change guru, Tom Peters, I stopped my presentation and asked, "What if Tom was here right now? What would he say you should do?" The discussion that followed "clicked."

→ Another time, while selling marketing research I shifted a presentation from describing how my audience could do a customer satisfaction survey themselves to a discussion of what makes customers satisfied in general. I reached the click point by sharing knowledge I had from previous experience working on dozens of customer satisfaction surveys. After the click point, we went back to my prepared materials, and suddenly they were excited to buy a customer satisfaction survey from me.

→ Once I discovered that several people in my audience shared a similar background to mine. We clicked by reminiscing for a bit about some shared experiences. Then I shifted back to selling by saying, "Hey, back then, I was just like you. And just like you are now, I thought these things didn't matter. But then I discovered …"

The Close

Visualize the Result. After you have brought your audience to a point of excitement, asking for action is often easy. If you are looking for a straight purchase or donation, an excited audience will often grant it just for your asking. But some excitement-based presentations are heavier on emotion than detail, and your audience may need help visualizing the final step.

Norwood Smith says he likes to use an imagination exercise to help his audience visualize the kind of behavior he is looking for. Smith meets with companies and associations and encourages individuals to speak up internally and suggest their national organization holds their next meeting in Tampa, Florida.

First, Smith gets his audience excited about Tampa as a destination. Then he asks them to imagine what they would feel if they had personally recommended the Tampa destination for a meeting that becomes a tremendous success. Says Smith, "Imagine what it would feel like to be enthusiastically thanked for speaking up when you did." Smith asks his audience to imagine this, and to speak up and recommend Tampa.

David Zaus, principal of Zaus Downes Inc., uses a different kind of visualization to move his presentations to commitment. Zaus Downes is a design firm specializing in retail and trade show displays. Often in meetings he can get an audience excited about a design strategy, but moving them to commitment is difficult until they can "see" what they are buying. Zaus is a skilled sketch artist who will actually stop his presentation to draw what he and his audience have envisioned. Says Zaus, "When they see a live drawing being created before their eyes, it's like magic and they think I'm a magician." If everyone in the room agrees that Zaus's drawing is on target, they are sold.

In short, if you prepare and share a meaningful presentation with passion and find a way to connect it to the needs and passions of your audience, something will "click" and result in excitement. And if an excited audience can see how to take advantage of what you have gotten them excited about, they will buy it.

3

The Presentation That Persuades with a Story

Storytelling reveals meaning without committing the error of defining it.—Hannah Arendt *(German-born American philosopher and political scientist; 1906–1975)*

We are lonesome animals. We spend all our life trying to be less lonesome. One of our ancient methods is to tell a story begging the listener to say—and to feel—"Yes, that's the way it is, or at least that's the way I feel it. You're not as alone as you thought."—John Steinbeck *(American novelist and writer, Nobel Prize for Literature in 1962; 1902–1968)*

Do not tell fish stories where the people know you; but particularly, don't tell them where they know the fish.—Mark Twain *(American humorist, writer and lecturer; 1835–1910)*

In November 1995, President Bill Clinton and the Republican-controlled Congress failed to reach agreement on a federal budget. Without congressional money came the first of two federal government shutdowns that temporarily curtailed government services and sent almost 800,000 workers home without pay. The shutdowns were a huge embarrassment for the Clinton administration, but polls at the time blamed the impasse on the Republican Congress.

Clinton fought back by sharing a persuasive story during his next nationally televised State of the Union Address presented to the full Congress. He began his story by introducing a man sitting next to his wife, Hillary, in the First Ladies Box:

> His name is Richard Dean. He is a 49-year-old Vietnam veteran who's worked for the Social Security Administration for 22 years now. Last year he was hard at work in the Federal Building in Oklahoma City when the blast killed 169 people and brought the rubble down all around him. He reentered that building four times. He saved the lives of three women. He's here with us this evening, and I want to recognize Richard and applaud both his public service and his extraordinary personal heroism.

The entire Congress, led by the Republican majority, gave Dean an enthusiastic standing ovation. Clinton continued his story, but with a zinger:

> But Richard Dean's story doesn't end there. This last November, he was forced out of his office when the government shut down. And the second time the government

shut down he continued helping Social Security recipients, but he was working without pay.

On behalf of Richard Dean and his family, and all the other people who are out there working every day doing a good job for the American people, I challenge all of you in this chamber: Never, ever shut the federal government down again.

Regardless of your own political viewpoint, you can see how this was a smart presentation strategy that Clinton used to turn the tables on his political rivals. After his speech, Clinton later wrote in his autobiography, "I didn't think I had to worry about a third government shutdown. Its consequences now had a human heroic face."

HOW THIS WORKS

Stories are great persuaders because they create a sympathetic emotional response with an audience. If you tell an audience about the most embarrassing thing that ever happened to you, every audience member, on some level, will be thinking either about an embarrassing moment of their lives or how they would feel if put into your situation. Clinton's story had huge impact as a national audience imagined what it could feel like to be a true patriotic hero like Richard Dean, suddenly tossed out of his job by a frivolous Washington power game.

Pitfalls

Thinking Your Personal Stories Won't Work Because You Don't Live as Interesting a Life as a Professional Speaker

Listening to a professional speaker like Emory Austin, president of Emory Austin and Company, can be intimidating. Austin is a master storyteller who inspires and motivates audiences as a professional speaker. Everyday events just seem to happen to her that result in fascinating stories. Most of us just don't lead as interesting lives. Or do we? I hope you will soon see that your own personal stories carry a unique persuasiveness. Assuming you have earned the right to stand before an audience, you have a lot to share that could be presented more dynamically in the form of a story. Also, much of a story's persuasiveness comes from how it is structured and delivered, not in how universally entertaining it is.

Thinking That Stories Are Just for Entertainment

An executive once told me that he did not have time to include stories in his presentation because he had so many charts and statistics to share. While a good statistical chart can be a great way to make a point, it is rarely a good way to make a point memorable or connected to an emotion. If your goal is persuasion, and not just throwing information at an audience, then stories need to be a part of your presentation.

Step by Step: Preparation

Start by Asking, "What Feeling Do I Want to Bring Out?"

Stories are emotional persuaders. To use them you need to think about the emotional response you want from your audience. Do you want to elicit pride in going along with your program, anxiety at the possibility of going with a competitor, excitement about choosing a groundbreaking course of action?

A well-told story can bring out any one of these feelings, but not all of them. You need to choose one emotion that will help your persuasive objective.

Look for Instructive Incidents

Persuasive stories are all around us every day. But we may not recognize them as such. They begin as everyday incidents that have a message, lesson, or humor. A persuasive storyteller recognizes the value of these incidents and will organize and structure them into a story with impact.

Recently a client confronted me with the news that a direct competitor, whose business was poor, had offered him dramatic discounts. I was able to overcome the possibility of losing business to this competitor by sharing a story. But my use of the story actually began more than five years earlier.

Back then, I was selling in the same industry but to a different account, ABCDigital Corp (not their real name). Again, I was in a competitive situation against a desperate discounting competitor. This time I lost the bid and ABCDigital began buying from this competitor. The more ABCDigital bought, the lower the prices went until eventually ABCDigital made this competitor their sole supplier. But when this supplier went bankrupt, ABCDigital started having major delivery problems. For six months they had shipping delays, and customer satisfaction dropped sharply. Several aggressive competitors took advantage, and they stole ABCDigital's five biggest customers. ABCDigital never recovered. They lost momentum, and two years later they filed for bankruptcy. At the time, I filed this instructive incident away and organized it into the story you just read.

When I shared this story recently, it had a huge impact on my audience. This was an industry-specific story, and most in my audience knew about ABCDigital, with several even knowing people who had lost their jobs when it went down. After my ABCDigital story, no one in that room was enthusiastic about taking a chance on another risky discounter. The most persuasive stories are ones that involve people, places, companies, or organizations with which your audience is familiar.

Start looking in the business environment you share with your audience for instructive incidents from which to build your stories. Also, look for stories from your personal life that you can share to communicate values and beliefs.

I like to take notice when someone changes their mind in a way that benefits my persuasive goals. For instance, there could be a great story in the making any time

→ A new customer decides to buy your product
→ An opponent changes her mind and supports your candidate
→ An organization changes direction to support your program
→ Someone in your personal life communicates or discovers something exceptional

Define the Main Character

At the heart of any persuasive story is a main character. When you share a personal story, that character is you. I often use stories of well-known industry or historical leaders. But it's not important that they are famous, as was the case with Clinton's Richard Dean story; what is important is that the story holds together and dramatizes the right message.

When freelance writer Steve Fayer began writing his treatment for the introductory program of *The Great American Depression* series for public television, he was looking for a way to dramatically connect all the facts and figures that led up to the Depression. Fayer knew that throwing facts and statistics at his audience would not achieve this. Through research, he discovered that in pre-Depression America, the auto industry "drove" prosperity, and Henry Ford drove the auto industry. Fayer placed Henry Ford at the center of his treatment and used him as the main character to connect all the events and facts with great dramatic effect.

Boil It Down

"Most stories start out too long," says Ann Bloch, professional writing coach and president of Ann Bloch Communications. She advocates writing out your story and underlining and keeping just the parts that *must* stay in. Work with those essentials and drop the rest.

Start with the Crisis Point

Bloch suggests that after you boil down your story, find the dominant emotion or crisis point and start telling your story there.

Says Bloch, "If you don't have a crisis point or a dominant emotion, you probably don't have a story and need to rethink if your incident is even worth telling."

Beginning storywriters are often fearful that if they give away the emotional high point of the story, there's no excitement or suspense for the rest of the story. Often the exact opposite is true. Bloch describes this approach as "the Hitchcock effect" because in most Alfred Hitchcock films, you know who has been murdered near the beginning of the film. Does knowing who was killed make the story less interesting? No, because soon you are riveted to the story to find out how it happened and who did it.

You should never be a slave to sequence. Bloch demonstrated this in a talk she gave at the National Speakers Association. She started with a sequential story,

> I want to tell you about my Uncle Jack. You wouldn't believe what a clever guy he was. He was born in Ohio in 1939. He spent the first years of his life on a farm....

Bloch paused, looked at her audience, and asked, "How are you feeling now?"

"Bored," came the response.

"Let's start the same story differently... My Uncle Jack was arrested in 1999 in New York City for attempting to walk a tightrope between the World Trade Center Towers. [pause] By the way, it wasn't the first time! Now, Jack was born in Ohio in 1939, and spent the first few years of his life on a farm...."

Now do you want to know more about Uncle Jack? You bet.

Replace Dull Words

Some words are just more colorful, funny, and dramatic than others. Go through your story and replace the static words. Changing one word can make a big difference.

Consider the Woody Allen line

I am thankful for laughter, except when milk comes out of my nose.

Why milk? Because milk is a funny beverage; it reminds us of childhood, innocence, and cows. Water is not a funny beverage; it's clear and commonplace. "I am thankful for laughter, except when water comes out of my nose" is not nearly as funny.

Add Illustration with Words

Master storyteller Emory Austin adds vivid visual images to her talks. Says Austin, "I tell my stories in a way that my audience can picture what I'm talking about. I like to say things like

"I remember just what that room looked like."

"I can remember exactly what it smelled like."

"Is there a place in your past that you associate with smells?"

"Go back and take a look."

Afterward, people come up to Austin and say, "I could see that room that you had to type letters in. I could picture all of it."

Add Illustration with Pictures

I illustrate stories I tell by using photographs to put my audience into situations we can discuss. To challenge an audience of sales trainees about their questioning technique I asked them to take an imaginary walk down West 57th Street in New York City. I illustrated the "walk" with photos I shot at eye level as I walked the same street. As my audience "walks," several passersby come up to them and ask them for directions. At each encounter, I pause the story and ask how they feel about answering the question for directions. I visually put my audience into the story, just like Austin does with her words.

Sharpen the Story

Sharpening a story with a message is the same as sharpening a funny story. Either way, a persuasive story has to deliver a message, a punch line, or both.

　　Probably the funniest story I ever told to an audience was from a real-life incident with my daughter Laura. As is often the case, when the incident happened there was no laughter or people telling me to "write that one down." But when I sharpened it and shared it at my daughter's Bat Mitzvah, it positively brought down the house:

> At age seven, my daughter Laura and I were walking back from a beach on Cape Cod. As we walked through the beach parking lot, we passed a huge black SUV with the back hatch open. Inside we saw a big metal tub full of freshly dug clams. Laura, who is curious and compassionate about all living things, had some questions for the clam diggers:

"Are they still alive?" Yes they are.

"How did you catch them?" We dug them up.

"What are you going to do with them?" We're going to cook them and eat them, and they're going to taste great!

Through her questions and enthusiasm Laura charmed the clam diggers who, to my surprise, offered Laura a clam to take home and eat herself.

Laura accepted enthusiastically, but she then paused for a moment and cautiously asked if she might possibly have another clam to keep the first one company for the ride home. The clam diggers chuckled and complied. After another beat, Laura asked if she could have yet another clam for her younger sister, Jenny. Then, she asked if she could have a companion clam for her sister's clam.

As Laura and I left the parking lot, her tiny hands could barely hold the four live clams.

In a deadpan voice she turned to me and said, "Well, I saved four, but the rest are goners."

Here is how to sharpen a story.

Write Out the Whole Story. Comedians and professional story-tellers can spend hours fine-tuning one sentence. If you don't write out your story, you won't be able to sharpen it.

Write the Punch Line. If one was not actually said in the story you need to write one. Find the wisdom, twist, surprise, zinger, moral, deeper truth, heartfelt moment, or piece of absurdity that makes your story funny or meaningful. Now condense and write it into a single sentence. If you don't think your humorous story has a punch line, rethink it, as it will not get a laugh. If your meaningful story does not have a message that can be condensed into a single sentence, you may not have a story worth telling.

Draw an Imaginary Line between the "Setup" and the "Punch." The "punch" is the line that delivers the meaning or laugh. In a funny story, this is called the punch line. In a meaningful story, I call it the "meaning line." The setup is everything that comes before this line. It is important to separate these two sections, so you can establish contrast between them and develop them separately. Some professionals actually draw a real line on paper between the two sections when they are developing this part of a story.

Set Up the "Punch." Expand and clarify parts of the setup that make the punch stronger, funnier, or more meaningful when it comes. Delete parts of the setup that do not add to the impact of the punch.

Here is an example of expanding a part of the setup: Every time Laura asked for yet one more clam her behavior became more pronounced, and thus funnier when the punch came and we realized she was acting not to accommodate her appetite but because of her love of all living things. So I expanded that part. I could have said, "Laura asked for and received four clams." But that would not have been as funny.

Here is an example of adding clarification: In this story, I added in the line "Laura, who is curious and compassionate about all living things." This narrative line occurred nowhere in the actual event. But I added it for clarity, since not everyone in my audience knew that Laura was an animal lover, and therefore might not get the punch line.

Add Exaggeration. When you tell a funny or dramatic story you are given some license to exaggerate. This is less so with stories about specific business issues where you need to be more factual, more so with stories that are told just to be funny or dramatic. Consider the meeting joke:

> "When I die I hope it is in a meeting…
> because the change will be so subtle."

It's humorous because it is exaggerated and overdramatic. Making things bigger, brighter, or darker than real life makes them funnier. In real life, the tub of clams in my story was in the back of a small, rusty station wagon. I made it a "huge black SUV" to make it seem more sinister, making Laura's victory sweeter, and the punch line funnier.

Rewrite the Punch or Meaning Line. The punch of a humorous or dramatic story needs to be short and quick, and it must deliver the payoff or surprise with emphasis. You need to put the "zinger" part of the punch at the end. In my clam joke, "In a deadpan voice she turned to me and said" came first, then afterward came, "Well, I saved four, but the rest are goners." It is just not as funny the other way around.

Step by Step: Telling the Persuasive Story
The Introduction

Actually, Stories Don't Need Introductions. You don't need to say, "I'd like to tell you a terrific story from my last Kiwanis Club meeting." If you do, some of your audience will start to think,

"Hey, so far this story is not too great." The fewer the expectations you set up in your audience's mind, the better. Just jump in and start storytelling.

Use a Story to Introduce Your Subject. I once heard Ron Wall, executive vice president of Ascend Media, use a short version of the story of Abraham Lincoln's life to introduce a talk on the need for persistence. Wall had slides that listed the milestones of the life of Lincoln without the president's name or dates on them. He began by asking, "How many of you know who this is?" Then he rolled the slides. The list of setbacks and tragedies in Lincoln's life before becoming president is truly amazing, and Wall's sharing them while holding back Lincoln's identity had his audience transfixed. When he finally revealed Lincoln's name to the audience, I heard a murmur of amazement ripple through the crowd. Wall had put his audience in the emotional mood to hear his message.

Invite the Audience Emotionally. Emory Austin recommends extending an emotional invitation. She asks, "Do you recall a time when you were overwhelmed by change?" By doing this she is not giving her story away; she is inviting the audience to be open to feel what is coming.

The Main Body

Telling a story is a performance. Most dramatic stories, intended or not, follow a three-act formula. While you don't need a curtain call between them, you need to make note of where they are so you can add dramatic emphasis as you tell your story.

The best definition I've ever heard came from Steve Fayer, series writer for the PBS documentary *Eyes on the Prize.* Fayer used the following definition of dramatic structure to guide his research staff while developing this series on the civil rights movement that became one of the most highly acclaimed television documentary series of all time.

"Act I – get your man up the tree."

Here you introduce your main character and his or her problem. When you tell this part of a story, describe the main character (or yourself if it is a personal story) in sympathetic tones. As you introduce the challenge, obstacle, or conflict, you need to act like the danger presented by the conflict is real.

"Act II – throw stones at him to the point where by the end of Act II you wonder if he is ever getting down from that tree."

The conflict develops to a point where resolution seems almost impossible. As you tell the story you need to keep up a feeling of danger if the problem is not resolved.

"Act III – get your man down from the tree."

This is where the emotional pay-off comes. Here your audience needs to feel elated, inspired, more confident, anxious, etc. The emotional result now needs to be tied to your persuasive goal.

Look Constantly for Audience Feedback. Telling a story is an interactive process. You need to constantly gauge the audience's reaction. Watch how attentive they are. Look for signs of confusion, introspection, or distraction. I like to look at faces of individual audience members, especially their eyes.

If you feel you are losing your audience, you need to make adjustments. Sometimes picking up the pace will bring them back. Just as often, to the surprise of many beginning storytellers, slowing down and adding more drama in the telling will bring them back.

Master storytellers go beyond just pace adjustments and edit their stories' content as they tell them, adding sections or dropping them in response to audience feedback. This is another reason why personal stories are so effective. If you lived it, you can often share different parts of the story based on how your audience is reacting.

Closing

When your story concludes, it is time for you to turn the story's emotional reaction into a persuasive event. You need to do two things quickly after the message line or punch line of your story is delivered.

First, you need to get agreement on what your audience is feeling collectively. If your audience members really thought about it, each would have a slightly different reaction to your story. To transform this moment into a persuasive event you need to move the group toward a consensus as to what they have just felt together. Most often a single sentence can accomplish this.

For my ABCDigital story, I used this line:

➡ "I think we all agree that buying from a low-cost supplier has big risks."

Other sentences can start with

➡ "Don't we all feel that…"
➡ "How can you not agree that…"
➡ "Aren't we all excited about…"

Second, once your audience has agreed on a group feeling, move to ask for action. With my ABCDigital story, when everyone nodded their head with my agreement line I asked for specific behavior, namely, not buying from another low-cost, high-risk competitor.

The key to using a story as a persuasive tool is to use it to bring out a strong emotion, then use the rest of your presentation to channel that feeling into a change of behavior.

4

The Presentation That Sells a New Idea

New ideas pass through three periods:
It can't be done.
It probably can be done, but it's not worth doing.
I knew it was a good idea all along!
—Arthur C. Clarke (science fiction author and inventor; 1917–)

The best way to have a good idea is to have a lot of ideas.
—Dr. Linus Pauling (American physical chemist and two-time
Nobel Prize winner; 1901–1994)

A committee is a cul-de-sac down which ideas are lured and then
quietly strangled.—Sir Barnett Cocks (author, long-serving
clerk of the British House of Commons; 1907–1989)

I had a monumental idea this morning, but I didn't like it.
—Samuel Goldwyn (producer; 1879–1974)

On March 19, 1999, Steve Forbes entered the crowded field as a candidate for the Republican nomination for President of the United States. There were nine candidates running, and Forbes's entry made it a field of 10. The son of publishing magnate Malcolm Forbes, Steve was little known in national politics, and most observers bet his only chance of winning would be after massive spending from his personal fortune. But the unique advantage of personally bankrolling a campaign vanished when rival candidate Maurice "Morry" Taylor, a millionaire wheel magnate from Quincy, Illinois, spent about $1.5 million of his personal fortune on TV ads in the early days of the campaign.

Despite the odds, Forbes shot past eight of his rivals in the first few primaries to become the solid second-place contender behind Bob Dole, the long-standing U.S. Senator from Kansas.

Most credit the success of Forbes's campaign to his ability to present new, compelling ideas that challenged his audiences. One idea, the flat tax, eventually took center stage and became almost synonymous with the Forbes campaign. *USA Today* reported, "Dole pokes fun at Forbes for being a one-note candidate: 'You ask him about your headache, he gives you his flat tax message.'"

The story of how Steve Forbes, a virtual political unknown nationally, could enter a crowded field and have a solid shot at winning the Republican presidential nomination is the story of just how powerful an idea, skillfully delivered, can be.

HOW THIS WORKS

The essence of using an idea to persuade is to sell an audience on a unique idea which, if accepted, gains acceptance for your candidate, product, or proposal. In short, buy my idea, buy what I am selling.

> **If you bought the idea of the flat tax back in 1999, you likely voted for Forbes. In the same year, if you bought the idea that the best value in computers was in buying direct from a manufacturer, you likely bought from Dell Computer.**

Pitfalls

Assuming That Everyone Loves a New Idea

In the early nineties I had a client who sold robotic camera systems for television newsrooms. The idea was to use emerging computer technology to robotically control the three cameras on TV news sets. Stations could preprogram camera moves into the system computer, giving them more predictable camera moves. Since TV news anchors don't move around much, this meant that one operator could now run all three cameras. This is a great idea, unless you were one of those camera operators.

"New ideas" often carry a romance. But every idea, when implemented, causes change that will disadvantage someone. To a TV station manager, paying fewer people to run studio cameras sounds like a great idea. To the camera operators who would lose their jobs… not so great.

Before you present an idea, think about whom your idea will disadvantage. You need to anticipate how to react if these people are present or represented in your audience.

Assuming That Everyone "Gets" Ideas at the Same Rate

I once tried to sell magazine ad space to a rep from a small manufacturer who was frustrated that they could not afford an ad campaign to compete with a much larger competitor. Their competitor ran full-page, full-color ads in trade magazines. I called my contact, said I had a great idea for them, and asked to make a presentation.

A week later I met with six people, who represented their entire sales and marketing staff. My idea was to run less expensive, small space ads more frequently than their competitor. By running more often with lower-priced ads, they would have ads in issues where their competition had no presence.

I laid out the theoretical plan and discussed how to construct smaller space ads so they would have the best impact possible. The reaction to my presentation was enthusiastic, and I was asked to call the next day for an order.

When I called, I was in for a shock. Somehow the message of "run more smaller ads to counterpunch your competitors' less frequent larger ads" got scrambled up to say "the smaller the ad, the better." My client told me they planned on not running any display ad space with me but would opt to run tiny classified ads in the classified ad section, which I did not even sell. "We were unanimous on this, Josh—after all, it was you who convinced us that the smaller the ad, the more effective it will be." Yikes! Don't quote me!

Ideas can be abstract until they are implemented. Sometimes after you leave the room, ideas can get reinvented to mean things about which you never dreamed. If you don't think your audience can handle abstract thinking, walk them through some implementation scenarios before you leave the room.

Thinking That All Ideas Sell

I had spent months convincing a client to sponsor a custom e-newsletter to be created by the publishing company I was representing. The company CEO had agreed to the project in principle, but it still needed a "great idea" to shape the content and finalize the deal. I arranged a conference call with the CEO, several of his operatives, and my publisher, an industry expert.

I introduced the session, and for the first 15 minutes I asked the CEO a battery of questions that got his people and my publisher up to speed on our discussions so far. Out of the blue my publisher shot out that he had a great idea. He proposed a series of newsletters to be created especially for new potential customers. The newsletters would be sent to prospects, one a week for six weeks, after a customer expressed serious interest in the company's services. My publisher got very excited about the idea and offered a lot of terrific insight into just how it could be structured and delivered. The CEO was clearly interested and the rest of the conference call focused on this idea.

The next day, the CEO thanked me for the conference call, and the idea. There was one problem though: there was really no reason for the CEO's company to need the resources of a publishing company to do this newsletter. The newsletter's content would be far better done by people in his own company who were more familiar with the steps of wooing new prospects, and delivery could go out more quickly if sent out by sales administration. There really was no way we could actually sell anything or bill anything if they used the idea. By selling this idea, good as it was, my publisher had pretty much killed the sale.

Before you start, ask, "If they buy my idea, will they buy what I am selling?"

Consider these four ways an idea most often results in a sale:

1. *Own the idea.* Steve Forbes "owned" the idea of the flat tax. If you wanted it as part of your future, he was the guy who could deliver and you had to vote for him.

2. *Sell an idea as feature.* In 2003 Seachange Technology introduced a new idea to structure video storage by using a ring

pattern instead of the commonly used linear structure. If IT audiences bought the idea of the ring structure, they had to buy from Seachange, the only supplier who had it.

3. *Stress your ability to do the implementation.* An ad agency recently proposed a new idea for a marketing campaign that targets senior citizens. Because the agency had extensive and unique knowledge and experience implementing programs like the one proposed, they felt confident they would get the contract if the client liked the idea. The client might say, "Okay, we love the idea. Who can make this happen?"

4. *Emphasize your specific expertise to deal with the change.* A technology company proposed using new digital technology to change the workflow at a radio station. While many suppliers offered the equipment necessary, implementing the changes in workflow required specific expertise that only this company could provide.

Ask yourself:

What idea can we advocate which, if accepted, generates preference for our product or service?

Step by Step: Preparation

Ask Yourself, "Has My Audience Heard This Idea Before?"

I once stood in front of an audience of 15 people and said, "I'm here to propose a new idea: building a streaming video section into your Web site to demonstrate new products." A tall man in the front row stood up and said, "We love that idea! We've been working on a streaming section on our Web site for weeks now. It should be posted next Thursday."

Asking a few questions before you arrive can prevent this experience from happening to you. But you don't want to give your idea away completely. I take an incremental approach and give up details of my idea gradually. For example, I might start by asking an open-ended question like, "I have an idea to help make your advertising more effective. Have you heard any proposals like that before?" If the answer is "no," I am home free. If they answer "yes," I would give up a little bit more. "My idea involves using fractional ads more aggressively than you might normally think of using them." Then I would say, "I have a way to make this work for your company's situation. Does this sound interesting?" I would give up a bit more detail but not propose the entire idea. Eventually if they really had heard an idea just like mine I would either find another idea or modify the one I was going to use.

I once gave a presentation on "Using Questions to Close More Sales" at a sales conference where another speaker had covered very similar material earlier that morning. But I was prepared. I had spoken with the earlier presenter, adjusted my talk, and began my presentation by saying, "I know you heard a lot about this subject earlier this morning, but I am going to approach it very differently." It's not terrible to present an idea that your audience has heard before, as long as you can provide different content or a different twist. The problem is being caught off guard.

Ask Yourself, "Is My Idea 'Audience Focused' or Just a Sales Pitch?"

Many presenters fail because they mistake a new idea on how their audience can buy for a real idea. I once heard a salesperson tell a customer, "We have a new product just out this month. It would be a great idea for you to buy it now since you can lock in a lower price for the year." But to an audience this is not an "idea," it's a sales pitch. To avoid this pitfall ask yourself these two questions:

1. "Is my idea about my audience's world or is it about my product?"

2. "Are the details I need to cover about the lives or experiences of my audience or are they product details?"

When Lee Iacocca told me about how he and his team at Chrysler came up with the idea to build the first minivan, he talked about the experiences of the American family in the 1980s. He mentioned how the baby boom generation was growing up and had kids, a dog, and more stuff to cart around. He did not talk about the engineering details of building a minivan.

It is often the experience of your audience that defines the need for a new idea. But you must define the idea in terms of your audience's experience, not in product details. An audience will buy an idea if it is about their life, business, hobby, or community. If it is about your product, then your "idea" may seem more like a sales pitch than a real idea.

Ask Yourself, "How Risk-Averse Is My Audience?"

When you sell an idea you are asking for change, and change involves some degree of risk. Some members of your audience will be thinking, "Okay, what this presenter says sounds good, but what if it doesn't work for me or us? What if something goes wrong?" Some audiences see risk as the fastest way to get ahead and stay there. Others see potential failure in every new venture.

I can always tell what kind of group I am dealing with by the questions they ask. When most of the questions are about potential gain, they are risk takers. When they ask relentlessly about potential dangers, they are not.

If I sense a layer of anxiety in my audience while presenting, I will often try to flush it out early in my presentation by asking a question in a half joking way: "Well how does this sound so far? Who's ready to take the plunge right now?"

Step by Step: Giving the Presentation

Get Attention

Ideas by their very nature have sizzle, so there is no need to add interest from unrelated jokes or stories. The best grabber you can use is to dramatize the benefit(s) of accepting your idea.

When Steve Forbes opened for the Republican presidential bid he announced,

> The theme of our campaign is very simple, and that is to make possible a rebirth, a new birth of freedom in America—freedom from the Internal Revenue Service. It's time to get the government back in the hands of the American people, to have a government that we can once again be proud of, instead of ashamed of.

Forbes further dramatized his opening by having the announcement carried live over the Internet, which was a political first back in 1999. He did not open with details about mending the tax code, or the accounting details of his plan. His introduction dramatized the benefits: restoring faith in government, growth in the economy, and economic freedom. It got attention!

Here are a few other ways to get attention right away:

→ *Ask, "What if?"* I once gave a presentation to an entrepreneurs club entitled, "Can you double the size of your business in one year by winning over problem customers?" I could have shared details of my problem client selling system, but the "What if" approach dramatized the benefit and grabbed their attention.

→ *Tell the idea origination story.* Every new idea has a story as to how it was conceived. Often this story tells how the idea arose to fulfill a need and explains its importance along the way.

In 1982, the idea for a new kind of computer company was started when a table of computer engineers sketched out on the back of a napkin a plan to build a computer that "just worked better." This origination story, communicated in a national ad campaign, helped sell the idea of using engineering smarts to deliver computers with superior functionality. As result, Compaq Computer went on an unprecedented growth spurt that made them the fastest-growing startup to reach the Fortune 500 list just four years later in 1986. Since most audiences would rather hear a dramatic story than an explanation, this approach can grab 'em.

→ *Tell the story of your own conversion.* A salesperson selling a new integration production started his introduction by saying, "Look, I used to be a widget buyer, and when Company X first approached me with a new idea for their product I thought they were crazy. Right now you might think it's crazy. But here is how I became a believer…" If the audience knows and respects you, this "personal" story can become an effective grabber.

Ask for "Idea Amnesty"

To present any idea powerfully you need to share it without interruption. If you are laying out something truly new, even well-intentioned questions will dilute the power of your initial presentation. There will be plenty of time later for questions.

To ask for "idea amnesty," say, "Please let me take the next five minutes to lay out the idea completely. After I do so, I'll be glad to take as many questions as you like." If someone jumps the gun and asks a question, say, "That's a great question, but please hold them until I explain the idea fully. Many of the questions you are going to ask will be answered if you allow me to finish."

Explain the Idea Clearly, Simply, and Briefly

This is not the time for dazzling graphics or clever repartee. The challenge is to present your basic idea in terms that are so simple that an eight year old can understand what you are saying. Very often diagrams, charts, or sequenced graphics can help do this. Ask yourself, "How can I verbally and visually present this idea so a child can understand it?" There are two ways to accomplish this.

Approach One: Baby Steps. I once won a large advertising contract from the General Motors (GM) account that my organization had previously failed to get when they used elaborate, detailed presentation materials. The problem was there were a dozen people involved in this evaluation; if even one of them did not understand the proposal, it would fail.

At the time I was reading Dr. Seuss's *One Fish Two Fish Red Fish Blue Fish* to my then-four-year-old daughter. It struck me that if I could capture the pacing and simplicity of that book for this presentation it might have a chance. Instead of explaining the concept in the three basic steps the content naturally flowed in, I stretched it to nine baby steps. I put each step on a single slide and wrote no more than two lines of explanation per slide. The leave-behind had the same structure as the presentation, nine pages with a simple content step on each one. The leave-behind really did read at the pace of a children's book. Throughout the presentation and in the leave-behind, I used words and language consistent with what a child would understand.

The presentation won the business from the GM account for the first time. In the end, it was not style, glitz, or showmanship that won the day, it was simplicity.

Approach Two: "It's Just Like What You Are Familiar with... Only Different." If your idea has parts to it that are familiar to your audience, why reinvent the wheel? Many audiences will "get" a new idea faster if you start with elements with which they're already familiar.

In the early day of the Internet, I made a presentation to a software company to use an e-mail blast, a service where my organization would send an e-mail to a list of recipients, to sell upgrades of their software. I told them, "For years you have been using direct mail through the post office to sell software upgrades to your customer base. Using an e-mail blast is very similar to this." Then I went on to explain what was the same and what was different about what I was proposing.

Offer Proof

Implementation of a new idea always means change. If acceptance means changing behavior, it's natural for your audience to expect some kind of proof. (More on using proof, see Chapter 7.)

Bring Up and Answer Typical Concerns or Objections

Before you open the room up for questions, take a preemptive strike and bring up anticipated concerns. For example, you can bring up cost objections by saying:

> Now, many of you might be concerned with the overall cost of this process. Before we open up for questions let me take a few minutes to address this…

I once presented a great idea to an audience that received it extremely well, except for one belligerent, extremely persistent, very vocal guy who brought up a routine concern and monopolized the dialogue for 15 minutes. My idea was nearly killed over an objection I could have diffused quickly before he opened his mouth. Don't let this happen to you. Before you open up a question-and-answer period with your audience, advance the selling dialogue as far as you can.

Closing

Getting commitment for action on an idea is different than closing a product sale. If your audience likes a product, there are channels to buy it. But ideas often need implementation. Forbes's flat tax would have needed a bill to be written, Congress to be negotiated with, a congressional vote, and so on.

Shift the Dialogue to Implementation

After you have answered all standing concerns, you need to move the dialogue from, "Should we do this?" to "How can we do this?" Simply look around the room and ask one of the following:

→ "Do we have a consensus that this is an idea worth doing?"
→ "Does everyone agree that this is a great idea?"
→ "Does everyone like what they hear?"

If everyone nods their heads or says "yes," then ask:

→ "What's the first step toward making this happen?"

Following this question, adaptive behavior should emerge.

→ "Do you need to form a committee or committees?"
→ "Do you need to approach management for a larger budget?"
→ "Do suppliers need to be switched?"
→ "Do individuals need to be assigned to certain tasks?"
→ "Do you need more research on competitors?"

Before you leave the room, your job is to assign specific individuals who can help implement your idea.

Adapt Your Idea and Give It Away

While selling market research, I once proposed a research study to monitor the brand perception of a company. An enthusiastic product manager asked if the same survey could carry questions that measured their customer service operations as well. I said, "Sure we can adapt the survey, that's a great idea *you* came up with." I adapted the survey proposal and started talking about the survey as though it was the product manager's idea. I gave "ownership" of the entire idea to him. Suddenly, it wasn't my idea, it was his and he would fight for it.

If there are modifications your audience members suggest, add the modifications and give ownership of the entire idea to those who suggested them.

Don't Be Proud

Most of the greatest ideas that I ever sold were cocreated with audiences during presentations. Most often I gave my idea's ownership away to my customers. It was no longer my idea, it was theirs. Ideas are among the most powerful of all persuaders; ironically, they are most persuasive when they are given away.

5

The Presentation That Persuades by Emotional Appeal

You can say the right thing about a product and nobody will listen. You've got to say it in such a way that people will feel it in their gut. Because if they don't feel it, nothing will happen.
—William Bernbach (Advertising executive who topped Ad Age's 2005 list of the 100 most important advertising people of the century; 1911–1982)

One of the common mistakes of mankind is to assume that men and women are actuated by the logical. They are not. They are moved by emotion, prejudices, all sorts of unreasoning and unreasonable considerations. That is one reason books are of so little help in selling. Books on salesmanship are generally logical.
—Specialty Salesman Magazine (January 1927, Edited by Robert E. Hicks, South Whitley, Indiana)

In this country, of course, great emphasis has always been placed on the individual. Personalities have always been more interesting to us than facts.—John F. Kennedy (U.S. president; 1917–1963)

By 1963 the American civil rights movement had gained enough political momentum to attempt passage of a national bill that would reverse local segregation laws throughout the country. The anticipated vote on this bill in Congress would be very close.

To motivate lawmakers on this issue and others, a great march on Washington was planned. Many politicians, including President John F. Kennedy, kept their distance, fearing political fallout if the march turned violent. As 250,000 peaceful marchers gathered in front of the Lincoln Memorial, Dr. Martin Luther King took to the podium to galvanize the marchers and motivate a wary Congress to pass the Civil Rights Bill.

King's famous "I Have a Dream" speech lasted less than 16 minutes and yet would go down as one of the most inspirational in human history. But at the time, some in King's organization worried that his presentation was an opportunity missed. King did not even mention the Civil Rights Bill. He shared no statistics and offered no proof to support the case for its passage.

But as the speech became widely reprinted and rebroadcast, those concerns began to fade. The appeal of King's presentation was emotional. Instead of making his case with facts, King helped a national audience *feel* what it would be like if the aspirations of the civil rights movement were realized.

Ralph Abernathy wrote in his autobiography, "Instead of dwelling on the bitterness of the past or the severe problems of the present, he gave the cheering crowd, as well as millions who watched on television, the vision of a future no one else had defined and few black people could imagine."

A great speech, but would it move the politicians to action? After the march, its leaders held a private meeting with President Kennedy. The president, who had distanced himself from the march at its inception, walked right up to King, greeted him with a grin and said, "I have a dream."

The Civil Rights Act of 1964 was signed into law about a year later, making it illegal to segregate any public facility anywhere in the United States or discriminate in employment on the basis of race.

HOW THIS WORKS

Emotions are an important part of any audience's decision-making process. They guide the decisions and can be the catalyst that makes those decisions happen more quickly. Addressing the emotional side of your proposal can help gain its acceptance.

Pitfalls

Thinking That You Can Create Any Emotion You Want in Your Audience

No one can create an emotion that does not already exist within the collective hearts of an audience. What you can do is to call attention to existing emotions, bring them forward and magnify them.

Trying to Figure Out How You Should Feel

The parts of your proposal you feel the most strongly about are the ones you will communicate most effectively. If you don't feel strongly about what you are talking about, talk about something else. I have never seen a presenter who could convincingly fake feelings all the time. If you fake your feelings while presenting, eventually you will get caught, lose credibility, and lose your audience. As Abraham Lincoln once said, "You can fool all of the people some of the time, and some of the people all of the time, but you cannot fool all of the people all of the time."

Step by Step: Preparation

It All Starts with the Audience

Ron Wall, executive vice president at Ascend Media, is a master at inspiring his audiences. According to Wall, all the magic begins with an understanding of his audience. "Before any presentation I ask myself, 'who am I talking to? What do they look like? What is going to strike their button?'" Although most of Wall's inspiring presentations appear to be delivered off the cuff, he says there is serious planning behind them all. "Once I understand who my audience is I start to think about what I can weave into the presentation that will be inspirational." Sometimes he will use a quote, a reference to someone's accomplishment, some humor, or a story.

Wall once joined me at a client dinner for 10 at a trade show. About halfway through the meal, the client's CEO started talking about the kind of company he had built and some of the positive values he had worked hard to instill in his organization. Throughout the CEO's talk, Wall listened carefully, trying to better understand the CEO and the others gathered at the table. Finding similar qualities between our own company and theirs, Wall launched into a stirring talk about how much we were alike. It's hard to describe the feeling around the table after his talk without sounding corny, but everyone at that table was zinged with a feeling of heart-felt camaraderie. By focusing on his audience and intuitively responding, Wall had done it again.

Take Emotional Inventory

Every product or option has an emotional component. Think about the feelings you have when you read the following brand names:

→ Coca-Cola
→ Dr. Pepper
→ Toyota
→ New York Yankees
→ Apple Computer
→ BMW
→ Sony

These brands have strong emotions associated with them. You can't turn them off in your mind if you try. Whatever you are presenting will also have some kind of emotional content associated with it. For a moment think about the emotions that different components in your proposal might elicit in your audience. If these feelings are helpful to your goals, then consider how they can be magnified. If they are not, you may need to redefine them for your audience. (For more on changing a perception, see Chapter 9.)

Think, "What Emotion Can I Bring Forward to Advance My Cause?"

Every movie shot today begins with a "storyboard," a sequential series of drawings, or frames, developed for each line of script to guide the cameraperson and actors.

Back when I produced television programs, I would work with a storyboard artist, who would draw those pictures. One of the key questions that needed to be answered as we began to visualize each frame would be, "What should this feel like?" The feel or mood of any frame could be altered with lighting, camera angles, and stage direction to the actors. With an understanding of the "feel" that was needed, my storyboard artist would develop the appropriate drawing.

As you look over the lines of your presentation script, you might ask yourself the same question: "What should this feel like?" When you plan a persuasive presentation, you need to plan the emotional content along with the informational content.

Ultimately when your presentation is over, your audience will have an overall feeling about what you have proposed. Your goal is for them to feel something that advances your proposal. Great emotional salespeople and presenters, like Ron Wall, intuitively read the feelings in an audience and then find ways to bring those emotions forward that will benefit their goals.

Assuming you know your audience, the next question to be answered is, "What feelings can I bring forward that will help my audience accept my proposal?" To figure this out, consider the following:

If my audience felt _____
about _____
they would (your goal here) _____

Here are some of the more common emotional responses that presenters bring forward:

→ *Likeability.* It's a proven fact that the more an audience likes you, the more likely they are to go along with your proposal. If the decision comes down to your proposal and someone else's, assuming that features and price are about the same, the person they like the best will always get the business.

→ *Anxiety.* Is your option perceived to be "safe"? Does not going along with your proposal involve risk? Does the alternative your audience is considering have scary aspects? Then bringing forward your audience's feelings of anxiety could help swing their decision to your product or option.

→ *Ego boost.* Does your product or option carry with it an emotional message of superiority, greatness, "being the best," or power? Then reinforcing this will help you win with ego-driven audiences.

→ *"I am so smart."* Is your option the "thinking person's" choice? Does your option or product take more sophistication to understand? Then emphasizing these aspects could help you win with people who perceive themselves to be smarter than average.

Other emotions commonly brought forward by presenters are optimism, hope, competitive winning, fear, and greed.

Emotional Honesty

Emotional honesty simply means representing yourself, your product or option, and your organization as they are, and not as you would like them to be to score an emotional point.

Let's say you are a homebody who loves nothing more than staying home on Friday night with a good book. But your audience is a pack of bar-hopping singles. Even though the last time you were even in a bar was five years ago at your high school reunion, it can be very tempting to talk up that experience to establish commonality with your audience. Unlike facts that can be checked, no one will be checking your bar-hopping history. But I say, don't do it. Presenting yourself like a bar hopper is emotionally dishonest, because it is not who you really are. You may win for the moment and temporarily create good feeling, but as your audience gets to know you they will figure it out and you will lose all credibility.

There are always ways to find commonality. But be emotionally honest and don't present yourself, your company, or your product or option inappropriately. In the long run it doesn't work.

Align Your Message and Yourself Personally

In 1997 Jerry White, executive director and co-founder of the Landmine Survivors Network, traveled to Stockholm to attend the award ceremony for the Nobel Peace Prize. White recalls an amazing event where some of the most esteemed world leaders spoke. That year Kofi Annan, Desmond Tutu, the Dalai Lama, Lech Walesa, and Elie Wiesel were all on the program.

As White watched the program he noticed that some of these amazing speechmakers were really connecting with the audience while others were just coming off as flat. It had nothing to do with the words; at this level, every speech in both content and words was perfect.

White observed that the speeches that really connected were ones in which "the message and the messenger were authentically aligned." For instance, when Desmond Tutu spoke, he was both messenger and message in one, because he was speaking from his own experience.

When you present your own product or option, if you can authentically align the message with yourself in a personal way, you will be more convincing. Tap into what it is personally that you share, experience, or deeply believe about what you are presenting. Ask yourself, "Is there a part of what I am presenting that I can be totally passionate about? Is there a part where I connect personally?"

Align Your Graphics

The graphics in your presentation carry an emotional message. If your graphics have a polished, high-tech look, this implies high-tech capability at your company. Pictures of people can add a more personal feel.

I once presented a proposal to a small, family-run business that was skeptical that I, working for a Fortune 500 corporation, could present a solution in which they would be interested. I intentionally gave my presentation a "homemade" look. The digital projector stayed back in the office that day as I walked my audience through pages on paper handouts.

Step by Step: The Presentation
Emotions Guide the Sale

According to Gerhard Gschwandtner, publisher of *Selling Power* magazine, emotion is the primary driver of the persuasion process on sales calls. Gschwandtner sees the persuasion process advancing as the customer makes a series of "emotional investments." Gschwandtner's first emotional investment involves the question, "Do I trust this person?" Trust is based on the feeling the customer gets from the salesperson.

The next emotional investment involves whether the customer feels the salesperson is competent enough. It will be hard for the salesperson to be persuasive if the customers do not feel

he or she can diagnose their needs and make useful recommendations.

Gschwandtner's next emotional investment is about the confidence the customer has in the company. If the customer does
not feel confidence in the company, the sale will not go through.

Finally, the customer will need to make an emotional investment to whether the product is worth the money.

These judgments are based on the feelings of a customer; the
feelings of an audience would be similar.

Present from the Heart, Not the Script

Rudolph W. Giuliani, former mayor of New York City, in his
book, *Leadership*, shared the story of how then-political consultant Roger Ailes (now CEO and president of FOX News) helped
then-mayoral candidate Giuliani prepare to present his case in
an upcoming debate.

> Whenever I'd prepare, I kept piles of books and position
> papers nearby, determined to have the answer to every
> question at hand. Roger was disgusted. 'Throw those
> damn books away. You already know more than you need
> to be a candidate, probably more than you'll need as
> mayor. Stop with all of this tax policy and crime policy
> and traffic policy. Do you think Mayor Koch knows all
> this stuff? Just get up on your feet, use the knowledge you
> already have, and you'll do a lot better.' As usual, he was
> right. He also taught me to communicate directly and
> with emotional honesty. When we shot our first few tel-
> evision commercials, I'd read them, as most candidates
> do. He told me, 'Forget it. Just take your glasses off and
> start talking, and we'll get it right. If you feel angry, com-

municate it. Sad, communicate it. Mopey, communicate it. Let people know that you're a human being and the rest will take care of itself.'

John Edwards, former Democratic vice presidential candidate, in his book, *Four Trials*, describes a similar lesson learned: "Today I give speeches on the Senate floor much as I presented my closing arguments as a trial lawyer. I don't read from a prepared text. Instead, I organize a body of ideas and then distill them down to a short series of points that I write out on a piece of paper, barely legible, even to myself. This approach doesn't always yield the most flowing rhetoric, but it allows me to speak to the jurors from the heart.... An artful and beautifully constructed closing argument read from a sheaf of papers is, in my view, just like the defense's parade of nurses each reciting the same speech. The perfection of it was alluring but it does not have the ring of truth to it. If I spoke directly and plainly to the jury, I could convey, however imperfectly, what I truly believed. And that is what I needed to do."

There is no emotion conveyed in a technically perfect speech that is read. To convey emotions you need to speak your own words.

Reading Your Audience's Mind with an Emotional Bounce

How can you read an audience's feelings strongly enough that you can respond to them and change direction if necessary? No one can really read minds, but intuitively many people use the "emotional bounce" technique to guide them.

Here is an example of how it works. I once had to present proposals for some online advertising to a very traditional company. As I prepared for the call, I wondered, was this the kind of traditional company that feels anxious when new things are presented? Or was this a company that liked to win and understood the need to take risks?

How should I play the emotional side? Present my online options as something safe, tried, and true? Or make it sound new, cutting edge, and maybe just a little dangerous… for their competition?

This was one of the oldest companies in the industry and its management had a reputation for being "old school." But I was getting a sense that the people in this room were excited about new and dynamic things even if they were a little risky. To test my theory, I did an emotional bounce. I faced my audience, smiled, and said in a jovial manner, "Hey, I know that your company was founded almost 100 years ago. I have to ask, is this stuff too far out for you?" The reaction was immediate. "Heck, no, we love it! We like this new stuff. Two years ago we got a new CEO who has been actively encouraging experimentation in new media." I did an emotional shift and presented my cutting edge proposal.

The key is to toss out a small comment, joke, or anecdote that gives the audience a chance to "bounce" or react, and you a chance to gauge their emotional reaction.

Change Direction to Increase Emotional Involvement

Dr. Martin Luther King's original script to his famous "I Have a Dream" speech had no reference to a dream of King or anyone else. King's speech focused on the challenges and grievances he and his audience were facing; near the end of the speech he concluded, "No, we are not satisfied, and we will not be satisfied, until justice rolls down like waters and righteousness like a mighty stream." The positive, hopeful imagery triggered a thunderous roar of applause. King skipped several paragraphs ahead into a section of his speech that would offer more of the same. While he was doing this, Mahalia Jackson, the famous Gospel singer who preceded King at the podium also sensed the change in the audience's mood. Jackson shouted, "Tell them about the dream, Martin," referring to a speech King gave the previous June in Cobo Hall, Detroit, where he had used the phrase "I have a dream" repeatedly. King continued with his prepared remarks for another few lines, when Jackson, again, called him to "tell them about the dream."

King left his prepared manuscript and began to improvise with lines from the Cobo Hall speech, "...even though we face difficulties of today and tomorrow, I still have a dream."

King recalled changing direction in his autobiography, "I had delivered a speech in Cobo Hall, in which I used the phrase 'I have a dream'... and I just felt that I wanted to use it here. I don't know why. I hadn't thought about it before the speech. I used the phrase, and at that point I just turned aside from the [prepared] manuscript altogether and didn't come back."

The most famous lines from one the most famous speeches in human history were added spontaneously in response to an audience's mood.

Closing

After you leave, emotions will play a part in your audience's decision-making process. Here is how:

→ *Emotions guide attention.* What you "feel" is important, is what you will focus your attention on. When you make a decision, the things you focus on become more important than things you choose not to focus on. Objecting to this idea, a member of a buying committee once told me, "Josh, when we walk into our committee we put our feelings aside and just evaluate the facts." But the decision of which facts were evaluated was probably guided by how they felt about them. By guiding your attention to subjects that you feel are important, your feelings can create a self-fulfilling prophecy where you buy what you initially prefer.

→ *Emotions are the basis for beliefs and values.* Often we formulate values from the emotional side of experiences. I once met a committee member who had been burned by several salespeople. The feelings that resulted from these experiences caused him to conclude that all salespeople are unscrupulous.

→ *Emotions are the basis for likeability.* People like to buy from people they like. If audience members feel you are friendly, optimistic, and someone they like, it can be a big help.

The time to ask for a commitment is when "it just feels right." With an emotional appeal, you might find yourself asking for commitment a bit differently than if you were using a more logical, persuasive approach. I once closed an audience with an emotional appeal by looking them straight in the eye and saying, "Doesn't it feel like we should do this?" Everyone nodded in agreement. We signed a contract later that day.

6

The Presentation That Persuades with Humor

Humor is more important than knowledge.—Albert Einstein (physicist; 1879–1955)

Comedy is very controlling — you are making people laugh. It is there in the phrase 'making people laugh.' You feel completely in control when you hear a wave of laughter coming back at you that you have caused.—Gilda Radner (actress, comedienne; 1946–1989)

Laughter is the shortest distance between two people.—Victor Borge (pianist, comedian; 1909–2000)

As President Ronald Reagan began his bid for reelection, he faced a growing liability, despite his enormous popularity. At 74, the oldest serving American president was rumored to fall asleep during cabinet meetings and some thought he might be slipping.

Reagan's first presidential debate against Democratic challenger Walter Mondale reinforced the problem. Reagan, "the Great Communicator," was off. He stammered, stuttered, and looked unsure of his answers. Soon after, reflecting a national concern, *The Wall Street Journal* ran a front-page story that asked the question: "Was Reagan too old to be president?"

While Reagan rehearsed for his second, and final, debate, one of his aides asked if he wanted to work up a response to the "age question," should it be brought up directly. Reagan smiled and said, "Don't worry fellows. I've got that one covered."

Early in the next debate, with an estimated audience of 100 million viewers watching, Henry Trewhitt, reporter from *The Baltimore Sun,* asked Reagan if he was up for the job of president despite his advancing age.

Reagan gave a half smile, cocked his head, and shot back, "Not at all, Mr. Trewhitt and I want you to know that also I will not make age an issue of this campaign. I am not going to exploit for political purposes my opponent's youth and inexperience."

Doug Gamble, a political and corporate humorist who was lead joke writer for Reagan at the time, recalls, "Mondale laughed, the audience laughed and the media panel laughed. That was the end of the age issue, the end of the debate, and frankly the end of the election. It all turned right there. Once age was taken off the table as an issue, there was no question that Reagan was going to win that election."

To the national audience unfamiliar with the use of persuasive humor, Reagan's superb delivery made the prepared quip look like the spontaneous response of a razor-sharp mind.

On Election Day Reagan won a landslide victory that carried 49 of the 50 states.

> **HOW THIS WORKS**
>
> A presenter who can make an audience laugh connects better and can make points memorable. But humor can be more than just a pleasant lubricant to the flow of information. In many "do-or-die" presentations I have given, humor was the defining moment because it has the power to temporarily arrest your audiences' critical thinking long enough for them to consider something new. Simply put, if you can get an audience to laugh at something, you can get them to rethink or change it. As the nation laughed at Reagan's age joke, somehow the "age issue" just didn't seem so important.

Pitfalls

Thinking That Spontaneous Humor Happens Spontaneously

Because the most common and effective way to include humor in presentations is to make it *seem* spontaneous, many people think it just pops into presentations without effort. This is an illusion!

Comedians who work with improvisational situations are required to read between seven and a dozen newspapers and magazines cover to cover each week. The great American humorist Mark Twain once quipped, "It takes me three weeks to prepare for a 30-minute impromptu speech."

Asking, "Should I Start My Presentation with a Joke?"

When you start off your presentation with an unrelated joke, then plunge into the content, humor may serve as a great icebreaker, but you have missed the opportunity to use it as a powerful persuasive tool. The question you should be asking is, "How can I use humor as a persuasive tool to advance my objectives?"

Thinking That You Don't Know How to Tell a Joke Because You Tried Once and No One Laughed

Doug Gamble faced a formidable challenge when approached by aides to George Deukmejian, then-governor of California. Deukmejian was known to the Sacramento press corps as one of the most lackluster speakers ever, and his aides wondered if Gamble could help.

One of the first questions Gamble says he asks when taking on new clients is if they are willing to poke fun at themselves. The governor reluctantly agreed to work with Gamble and cautiously approached his first attempt at humor. Gamble had provided lines like, "I understand that you have been searching for a speaker who can dazzle you with his charm, wit, and personality. I'm pleased to be filling in while the search continues."

The lines were especially funny coming from a politician with a reputation as a dry speaker, and Deukmejian came away from his first use of Gamble's preparations with a huge laugh. Advises Gamble, "For speakers and politicians, laughter is addictive. Once they hear an audience laughing at a joke that they've done, it's like eating just one peanut. Once you start, it's hard to stop."

It is not necessary to be a great comedian to use humor. What you need is a willingness to find your own way to use humor.

Thinking That Persuasive Humor Is Just about Jokes

In my early years as a presenter, I found joke telling intimidating but found a way to use humor frequently by showing funny pictures that I would doctor up and present in sequence. Besides jokes, you can add humor by using your own personal funny stories, showing cartoons, or sharing a funny story about someone in the audience. Besides poking fun at yourself you can poke fun at the boss, the audience, others in the room, your competition, or the town or building in which you are located.

Step by Step: Preparation

Identify the Point of Change

In every persuasive presentation there is a point at which you ask your audience to change. The closer you can get humor to that point of change, the more persuasive it will be. Through luck, Reagan was given an opportunity to make an age-related joke when he needed to neutralize the "age issue." But persuasive humor is more often planned.

I once gave a competitive sales presentation to a client who was splitting his magazine's ad space between my publication and a competitor, *AV Technology*. But my company had initiated new online advertising options of which I wanted my client to take advantage. When I was told that the overall ad budget could not rise to accommodate these new options, I targeted the dollars now being spent on my competitor, *AV Technology*, as my only hope.

In the past, when I had explored having *AV Technology's* budget cut back to fund my latest scheme, I was immediately rejected. The problem was that my client had a long-standing relationship with *AV Technology* that would make it personally uncomfortable to cut them back.

But the magic of humor is that it temporarily suspends an audience's analytical, mental mechanisms. While they laugh they are not thinking about cutting back *AV Technology* or what it might feel like to make the phone call that does it. And so, for a few minutes after I made a related joke I was able to get my message through.

I began with a PowerPoint presentation that outlined our new online options. Several of the slides sparked interest with the audience. I left the last slide, which listed all the online options, on the screen and continued, "I've heard strong interest for several of these. What you might not realize is that you can afford all the ones that you are interested in."

Then I turned to Jim, the vice president who managed the budget, and said, "Fortunately, you have a man of foresight in your group. Jim must have envisioned these new opportunities would emerge in the online world and over the past few years has been actually setting aside 'unused' advertising dollars for just this purpose."

Jim took the compliment well but looked confused and shot me a look that said, "What are you talking about?" The other six people in the room turned to Jim for an explanation. He just shrugged. Looking at him with a half-grin I said, "You know, Jim, those unused ad dollars you've been storing in the budget every year in the column labeled, [pause] *"AV Technology."*

The room erupted in laughter. Jim was relieved to be off the hook as the other people in the room realized my ruse of calling ad dollars spent on my direct competitor as "unused." I quickly shifted to a serious tone and pointed out the advantages of shifting the dollars: less duplication, a whole new approach, and so on.

By placing humor at the point of change, I had helped my audience temporarily slip past the uncomfortable thought of cutting back business with a long-standing supplier. In the end, they did cut back *AV Technology* by half to fund a new online program.

Your first step, then, is to identify the point of change in your presentation and to think about adding humor at or near that point.

Find Material

It is not hard to find humor. Every bookstore has a humor section with books that organize their jokes by subject. Type the word *jokes* into your favorite Web search engine and dozens of joke sites loaded with humor will appear. Personally, I have a joke book collection of over 40 titles, store jokes that people e-mail me in several Outlook files, and take a camera everywhere I go to snap pictures of funny sights.

It's important to develop an eye and ear for what is funny as it relates to your kind of audience and your kind of content. Sensitize yourself to notice what kinds of jokes your audience laughs at and organize yourself to collect some. I give a lot of presentations in the sales and marketing field, so I'm always looking out for joke books, cartoons, funny quotes, and stories having to do with salespeople or the persuasive process.

The best humor comes from your own experiences. If you are presenting to a certain audience type, chances are good that in your position or experience there are some funny occurrences that can be shaped into humorous anecdotes. When something happens to you that is funny, write it down.

Finally, as your presentations begin to create a more playful atmosphere, audience members may start sharing their own jokes and funny stories with you. Write them down!

Adapt or Localize Humor

I recently got a big laugh while presenting to a group of media sales reps by adapting a joke. My presentation was on how to get your sales message to reach the higher echelons in media buying organizations, even up to the illusive, hard-to-reach media supervisor at major advertising agencies. I started with a question, "How can you tell the difference between a media supervisor and God?" [pause] "It's very simple. God does not think he is a media supervisor."

I confess, I got this joke from a book of lawyer jokes, and I switched out the word *lawyer* to *media supervisor*. Was it funny? Maybe not to everyone, but to a room full of people struggling every day to get through to media supervisors, it definitely was.

You don't have to find jokes that are universally funny, just ones that are funny for your audience. Your challenge is to find humor that can be adapted to your audience's collective sense of humor. There is a lot of truth to the Bob Hope line, "A comedian is a man who originates old jokes."

Sharpen It

Stand-up comedians refer to a joke as having two parts: the "setup," which describes the situation, and the "punch," or punch line, which adds the surprise, twist, or payoff that gets the laugh. For example:

Setup: Change is inevitable …
Punch … except with vending machines.

Often you can make the joke funnier by separating these two parts and emphasizing lines in the setup that makes the punch funnier when it comes. For more about effective use of humorous stories in presentations, see Chapter 3.

Prepare Savers

As any comedian knows, not every joke works. But you can still get a laugh by using a saver, a piece of self-deprecating humor you share after telling a joke that bombs.

The late Johnny Carson was a master of the saver. Said Carson after a joke bombed, "Is there a revolver in the house? [after nodding acknowledgment that there was] "Hey, I'm going to keep plugging ahead."

Here are a few more savers:

→ "Some of you in the rear might not be able to hear me. After that joke, those of you in the front may want to go back and join them."

→ "That's the last time I buy a joke from [president of the association or company to which you are speaking]"

→ "Excuse me. For those of you who weren't paying attention that was a joke… I'll try another one later to see if you are paying attention."

Professional public speaker Lilly Walters wrote a whole book about savers called *What to Say When You're… Dying on the Platform.* Some of her better lines include

→ "That's what I call a quiet joke which is supposed to get a quiet laugh…. I guess it worked."

→ [to the only person laughing at your joke] "Could you turn around and tell that joke to the rest of 'em so they get it?... [pause] Thanks, Mom."

Prepare Your Delivery

1. *Practice.* Before you stand up in front of an audience, you must practice your joke. Give it in front of a mirror so you can see how it looks. Then try it out on anyone who will listen.

2. *Memorize your punch line.* Your punch line is too important to be left to chance. If you get distracted and blow the punch line, you have botched your whole joke. Memorize your punch line so you can recite it even if a fellow presenter slips and pours ice water down your back.

3. *Deliver the key phrases in your setup slowly and clearly.* If you watch Ronald Reagan deliver the key phrases of his setups, you will see that he slows down his pace almost as if he is reading to a child. But to compensate, he gives more facial and vocal expression. When you watch casually you don't notice, but the emphasis gets made.

4. *Let people know the punch line is coming.* The most common way to do this is to pause slightly before you say it. Comedian Joey Adams shares a few other ways: "Most comedians or professional storytellers have a trick giggle or clear their throats before or after the punch. Some waggle cigars or flick the ashes off their cigarettes. One stamps his foot, another slaps his thigh or claps his hands. Some just pause for the slightest moment—to let the audience know that the punch line is coming or gone."

5. *Deliver the punch line clearly, slowly, and plainly.* If they don't get the punch line, they won't get the joke. Make sure everyone in the back row can hear it.

6. *After you deliver the punch line, stop talking and wait for the laugh.* Sometimes it takes a few seconds for the joke to sink in. To a presenter, laughter is group behavior that needs to be encouraged. If you are home alone watching a funny TV show you don't laugh out loud nearly as much as when you are part of an audience or group. The best way to assure more laugh-out-loud laughter is to encourage it when it comes.

7. *Rethink.* Developing humor and a humorous style comes with time. Keep the jokes that worked, rework the ones that didn't. Don't blame the audience if a joke bombs.

"Setup and Punch" Visuals

The same "setup and punch" format that works for jokes and stories works for visuals as well: Before presenting to an audience of salespeople at North American Van Lines, I went to a truck stop and photographed some of their vans as well as some of their arch rival competitor's, Untidy Van Lines [not their real name]. On one of the "Untidy" photographs, I "Photoshopped" about half a dozen zany-looking gorillas scampering madly around the van.

At my presentation, I followed the same setup and punch formula:

Slide one: An Untidy Van Lines vehicle at the truck stop

Me: "Incidentally… on my way out here today I saw one of your competitors parked. It looked like the tires were a little low. But I soon found out that their real problem was not in their tires…"

Slide two: Untidy Van with half a dozen gorillas scampering wildly around

Me: "…have you seen their drivers lately?"

It brought down the house.

Step by Step: Giving the Presentation

The Introduction

Don't say, "I'd like to tell you a joke." Just jump into it and put the element of surprise to work for you. The kiss of death is to tell an audience you are about to tell a funny joke or story. Suddenly your audience is waiting for a great laugh. You've raised expectations, which will turn negative if they are not met.

The Main Body

Use Humor to Introduce Yourself. Audiences immediately take to *SellingPower* magazine publisher Gerhardt Schwantner when he begins by poking fun at his noticeable Austrian accent. But his audience has heard that accent before, as it sounds just like Austrian-born actor-turned-California-Governor, Arnold Schwarzenegger. Says Schwantner, "When I speak, I have an accent like Arnold, so I tell my audience I have a lot in common with Arnold. He says, 'Calyfornia,' and I say, 'Calyfornia.' But that is not all. I come from a little town in Austria and went to school there… and so did Arnold. And there is more. His father was a policeman who played the trumpet, and my father was a postman who played the violin. The only difference is that he speaks English with a funny Austrian accent and I don't."

Use Humor to Introduce Your Subject. Having worked with Jim Dickson, vice president of national accounts at The Inspiration Network, I know him to be one of the funniest people alive. But cable system operators who meet with Dickson for the first time often assume that, since he works for a faith-based TV network, he might be on the serious side. Dickson loves to shatter that illusion by introducing his subject with a laugh. As he introduces his cable TV network he informs them, with a twinkle in his eye, that his cable network is "the only one they are considering adding to their lineup that was anointed by God."

Use Humor to Reinforce a Key Point after You Have Made It. Says Doug Gamble, "I go through the speech or presentation trying to insert what has become known as 'sound bites,' bits of humor that will reinforce a point that the speaker is making in a creative and memorable way. If a joke won't do, sometimes it can be just a catchy line." Any point reinforced with humor becomes more memorable.

Use Humor to Diffuse Anger or Hostility. Abraham Lincoln, while on a campaign stump, was once accused of being two-faced by a heckler. He diffused the anger immediately by motioning toward his face and replying, "If I'm two-faced, would I be wearing this one?"

Use Humor to Reinforce Your Key Benefit. While Nigel Spratling, a technology marketer, was working for a technology company whose prime benefit was reliability, he created a trade show booth that looked like a small Polynesian village staffed with employees in Hawaiian shirts. Within the booth, Spratling placed a stage with a small beach, sand and all, where a humorous presentation was delivered by a relaxed-looking engineer sitting on a deck chair with a Mai Tai in his hand. Two attractive, Hawaiian-costumed women turned the flipchart while the engineer presenter commented that he used to be a worried engineer too. But ever since he discovered this company's reliable products, he has been able to relax and kick back...

Use Humor to Diffuse Criticism. When *Folio* magazine publisher Tony Silber was starting his own magazine, he had an exciting story but no money for a fancy media kit. Media kits, the information packet that tells a magazine's story to potential advertisers, are often elaborate and expensive. Silber's kit was just photocopied pages placed into a bright red generic folder bearing the name of Staples, the office supply store from which he bought it. To diffuse potential criticism, Silber poked fun at it. While feigning the tone of a temperamental design artist, he would say, "I actually had a lot of choices here and I really like the way the cover design came out. You see—I could've gone with blue, white or gold."

Closing

A well-placed laugh just before you ask for change or commitment can lighten the mood and make accepting your product or option easier. If the decision to accept your product or option is close, humor can make a big difference.

However, the first time your audience hears a joke from you should not be at the point of commitment. It will seem odd and awkward just popping up at the end. Also, there are serious-minded audiences who do not appreciate humor when they are considering commitment. For them, this is a serious time and not appropriate for jokes.

When you use humor at the close, it cannot be forced or seem like a manipulative "technique." I find that including humor is easiest and most natural during the summary just before you ask for commitment. Here, you typically review the points that scored well with your audience. As you cover these points I also review humorous incidents that occurred during my presentation. I make mental note of anything funny or awkward that happened and share them in my summary.

Mark Davis was a beloved but tough-as-nails division manager who invited me to present a series of training options to his group of sales managers. It was fortunate that he was not present at the time because when I mentioned a training session on selling extremely difficult customers based on my book, *Tough Calls*, Bob Morgan, obviously one of the most popular managers in my audience, cracked everyone up by blurting out, "Hey, I know a tough call. Mark Davis is coming here next month. I say we all take that course before he gets here!"

In my summary that day, as I began to list the training options that had generated interest with this group I turned to Bob Morgan and said, "And let's not forget that course on selling difficult customers. Bob, why was it you needed to take that class again?" My audience laughed, and humor was introduced just seconds before I asked for commitment for them to buy the "Tough Calls" training session along with three others. They bought.

Humor is more than a presentation icebreaker; it is a powerful persuader that works in a variety of ways. Humor has the power to break through skepticism, diffuse critical thinking, and help an audience let down their defenses, build a sense of humanity for the presenter, and make key points of a presentation memorable. If these are goals of your next persuasive presentation humor can help close the sale.

7

The Presentation That Lays Out "The Facts"

I am a firm believer in the people. If given the truth, they can be depended upon to meet any national crisis. The great point is to bring them the real facts.—Abraham Lincoln (American president; 1809–1865)

It is not the facts which guide the conduct of men, but their opinions about facts; which may be entirely wrong. We can only make them right by discussion.—Norman Angell (British economist; 1872–1967)

Get your facts first, then you can distort them as you please. —Mark Twain (American humorist, writer, and lecturer; 1835–1910)

I have a theory about the human mind. A brain is a lot like a computer. It will only take so many facts, and then it will go on overload and blow up.—Erma Bombeck (American humorist, 1927–1996)

A month after the shocking death of Princess Diana in August 1997, representatives of 86 countries gathered in Oslo, Norway to draft the final version of an international agreement to ban landmines.

At the start of the conference *The Economist* reported, "Quite a few countries might have been unrepresentative in Oslo had Princess Diana's gallant anti-landmines campaign not made it politically awkward for their leaders to stay away."

But despite the high moral ground, Princess Diana's campaign had not always gone smoothly. She began in January 1997 with a visit to Angola. In hospitals and villages, as she posed with child and adult landmine victims, her unrivaled publicity power sent shocking, heart-wrenching images around the world.

Her critics back in the United Kingdom were unmoved. They called her a "loose cannon," arguing that landmines were a practical defensive tool and that the princess was "uninformed." To respond to her critics and advance her cause, Princess Diana shared her thoughts on her Angola trip in a rare presentation given at the Royal Geographical Society in London.

To the surprise of her critics, Diana did not play the emotional card. There were no devastating stories of the victims she had met, no descriptions of the emotional angst of the trip, no photos of her standing beside children with mangled bodies. Instead, she said simply, "I visited some of the mine victims who had survived, and saw their injuries. I am not going to describe them, because in my experience it turns too many people away from the subject." Then she turned to "the facts" and they proved devastating enough:

Landmines are a worldwide threat.

Landmines cause 800 deaths and 1,200 additional injuries per month.

Angola has been devastated by landmines.

...a country where there are 15 million landmines in a population, Ladies and Gentlemen, of 10 million... In Angola, one in every 334 members of the population is an amputee.

Landmine use is based on a false economy.

Each victim who survives will incur lifetime expenses for surgery and prosthetic care totaling between £2,000 and £3,000. That is an intolerable load for a handicapped person in a poor country.... Many of these mines are relatively cheap—they can be bought for £5 apiece, or less. Tracing them, lifting them, and disposing of them, costs far more—sometimes as much as a hundred times more.

According to Jerry White, director of the Landmine Survivors Network, who helped introduce the princess that day and whose group cosponsored the event, "People were riveted by her presentation even with the distraction of the constant clutter and clatter of the photographers. Princess Diana let the facts speak for themselves. They were stark and powerful, and people reacted emotionally to them. She was understated, but when you hear there've been thousands of children injured it has a powerful effect. The sheer numbers shock you."

A week later, Prime Minister Tony Blair reversed his government's position on landmines and joined Diana's crusade. In December 1997, an agreement to ban landmines, drafted in Oslo, with 86 countries represented, was signed into effect by 125 countries.

HOW THIS WORKS

Every human being likes to make up his or her own mind. The tremendous appeal of a fact-based presentation is that you ask your audience to come to their own conclusion based on a sequence of facts that you present. As a popular news network once sloganed, "We report, you decide."

Pitfalls

Thinking Your Facts Are Unshakable

For every unshakable fact you can present to support your case, there is a countervailing fact. Princess Diana's opponents cited the fact that landmines saved many servicemen's lives, as they offered a deterrent to attackers. Airing your facts is only part of the process. You also have to prove them and present them persuasively.

Forgetting Proof

In your own thoughts, a "statement of fact" is something you can say that you believe is true. But to a skeptical audience, your "statement of fact" is only a "statement of your opinion" until you prove it to them and they accept it.

Many facts do not require proof. If you were to say, "There are 24 hours in a day," there is no debate. But typically the facts that support the persuasion process are open to more interpretation. Consider:

→ We have the best IT solution for midrange companies
→ There will be an increased demand for single-resident apartments in Tokyo
→ Vanilla is America's favorite ice cream flavor

Statements like these only become "facts" when they are proven and accepted by the audience. Often the persuasion comes more from the proof than the statement itself.

Please consider that last statement:

Vanilla is America's favorite ice cream flavor.

I could "prove" this statement by using retail sales records as reported by the International Dairy Foods Association:

Through February 2003, major food retailers in the United States reported the following percentages of ice cream sales:
→ Vanilla: 33 percent
→ Chocolate flavors: 19 percent
→ Nut/caramel: 7 percent
→ Neapolitan: 5 percent
→ Strawberry: 4 percent

It's strong proof. Are you convinced?

But I could also argue that vanilla is not a "favorite" at all but just a "utility flavor," used frequently to top apple pies and bakery desserts, or in drinks like my cousin Ellie's amazing iced coffee punch with huge delicious scoops atop. More vanilla ice cream may be sold, but chocolate is really America's "favorite" flavor.

To prove this, I did several word searches on the U.S. Google search engine and recorded the number of hits each flavor had received:

→ "Chocolate ice cream": 2,450,000 hits
→ "Vanilla ice cream": 1,090,000 hits

Chocolate ice cream is clearly on more people's Web sites and minds. And furthermore:

→ "Chocolate enthusiast": 198,000 hits
→ "Vanilla enthusiast": 58,400 hits

Clearly we are more enthusiastic about chocolate.

→ "I love chocolate": 6,210,000 hits
→ "I love vanilla": 1,810,000 hits

Vanilla is fine on pie, but chocolate is what we love.

Do you still believe vanilla is America's favorite ice cream flavor?

If your opinion shifted even slightly as you read the last few paragraphs, please consider that it was not the statement of fact that changed your mind, it was the proof.

Step by Step: Preparation

Ask Yourself, "How Will the Audience Make Their Decision?"

A presentation that persuades by "laying out the facts" succeeds by building a step-by-step sequence of accepted facts that lead to a logical conclusion. The facts you choose must be selected with an understanding of how your audience will make their decision on what you present.

I was once preparing a competitive presentation for a technology company that was looking to narrow its current list of three suppliers down to two. The company had set up a "dog and pony" show where I, and two of my competitors, would present to keep their business. Assuming that this presentation would go as recent ones, I began researching facts that supported my case against the lead competitor. But a friend who worked at the target company tipped me off that this competitor had already been unofficially given the nod to continue as a supplier. Said my friend, "Josh, don't waste your time shooting at them, they are already on the plan." I immediately shifted to find facts that supported my case against my secondary competitor—and was successful in keeping the business.

In hindsight, it did not matter how well I prepared or presented the facts against my lead competitor. Even if I had spent twice the time preparing, that effort would not have won me the business. Had I not asked questions about the decision-making path my audience was on, through both official and unofficial sources, and selected my facts accordingly, I may not have been successful.

Before you start planning your presentation, find out as much as you can about how your audience will make their decision about what you are presenting. Find out:

→ Will they decide by consensus, organizational hierarchy, or as individuals?
→ How have they made similar decisions in the past?
→ Who are the key influencers and what do they believe?
→ Are there any key influencers who will not be in the audience?
→ Do they like a lot of details or are they "big picture" people?

→ How many products or options will they choose?

→ What is the time frame of their decision?

→ What are the key factors that will help them decide?

Immerse Yourself

In the fashion world they say that "clothes make the man," but in the presentation world it is the facts. Your audience will decide if you, as a presenter, are credible enough to persuade them. Your command of the facts, more than any other factor, will determine their judgment. Every audience has a reason for coming together that is surrounded by a body of information and facts. If you are presenting to diamond merchants, they will know a lot about diamonds. At some point, every member of that audience will ask, "She sounds good, but does she know enough about diamonds to really know if this is right for us?"

To win a favorable judgment, immerse yourself in the information world of your audience. Before I spoke to the sales staff of North American Van Lines, I researched Web sites, visited a truck stop, and interviewed several industry people. The more facts you find, the more from which you can choose.

Confessions of an Information Chameleon. After having worked in the trade magazine publishing industry for 20 years, I have learned to become an information chameleon. One year I worked on trade magazines in the computer, law enforcement, and video technology industries. I would go to trade shows and have to talk convincingly to companies that made mouse pads, video monitors, and bulletproof vests. I found that in every industry, at a given time, there are three facts about which the people who "know the business" are discussing. If you can find out what they are and share them, you can build credibility quickly. Currently

I am involved in a property in the emerging digital signage market. At this moment, the three facts you need to say are

1. Partnerships are essential in this market.
2. This market is expected to grow by 300 percent in the next two years.
3. Digital signage is a rapidly growing market but not yet a real industry.

Lay Out a "Trail to the Sale"

A fact-based presentation follows a logical path. Start with the conclusion at which you want your audience to arrive and back up a logical series of facts to where they are today.

Princess Diana did it in three steps:

1. Landmines are a worldwide threat.
2. Angola has been devastated by landmines.
3. Landmine use is based on false economy.

Conclusion: Let's ban landmines.

The logical structure is typically simple:

→ Introduction
→ Fact #1
→ Fact #2
→ Fact #3, etc.
→ Close

Often, if you look at the most persuasive facts you have, a logical sequence suggests itself. But sometimes that sequence is not obvious. When that happens, I try a negative approach. I flip my point of view and start from the premise that my product or option is wrong for the situation. Then I map out a sequence of facts to counter the negative case, fact by fact.

For instance, I recently gave a presentation to a group trying to sell them a sponsored Webcast that began:

> There has been a lot of negative talk about using sponsored Webcasts to improve business in our industry. I know there have been some recent failures that everyone has heard about. But Webcasts can also be tremendously valuable. I would like to show you point by point how those failures occurred and why I believe sponsored Webcasts can still be of benefit to your organization.

I took on the negative points one by one, then went on to show the value of a sponsored Webcast. I made the sale.

Ask, "Will It Persuade?"

Fact-based presentations are most often won in preparation, not at the podium. Before I stand in front of my audience I always take some quiet time and imagine what it would be like to be the most skeptical audience member watching the presentation of my fact sequence. I ask myself:

➙ *Are my facts enough about their situation and not just about my product or option?* Facts about your audience's specific situation will always be more persuasive than facts about your product or option. You need a balance of both. If your presentation is just about your product or option, go back and find some facts that are about their products, competitors, challenges, enemies, heroes, leaders, values, hopes, or goals.

→ *Will my proof hold up?* To convert the nonbelievers in your audience, you need to offer proof that is credible.

→ *Have they heard this all before?* If you have assembled the basic facts that support your case in a logical way, there is a danger that your audience has heard your story before. Make sure there is something new or different in your presentation that your audience has not heard before.

Bob Lipp, CEO of Better Business Presentations, helped a small software company achieve a huge win by coming up with a new set of facts for their presentations. Lipp found their current presentations primarily focused on their products and features. But in this software niche everyone was making features claims. Looking further, Lipp advocated using facts about the company's blue-chip customer and partnership lists. The result of this shift was immediate and unexpected. Sales rose dramatically and the company attracted so much attention that one of the largest software companies in the world made an offer to buy the entire organization.

Ask, "Is It Interesting?"

The real masters of fact-based selling develop an intellectual curiosity about their subject matter that compels them to understand and dig beyond the basic facts that support their case. They add facts that add perspective, fun, and interest.

During the recession after 2001 I gave many presentations to salespeople on "Selling though a Slump." To inspire my audiences to fight their way though a sluggish economy I researched information on how salespeople in the 1930s succeeded while selling during the Great American Depression. I opened my presentation with four stark black-and-white period photos, each with a fact or statement across the top:

Slide 1:
During the 1930s Depression:
Industrial output: down 50 percent

Slide 2:
Unemployment: 25 percent

Slide 3:
Stock exchange: Trading at 10 percent of recent value

Slide 4:
Here's how they did it then…. You can do this today!

Those facts put in perspective what selling in far worse circumstance was possible. My audience of salespeople selling in a recession was riveted from that moment on.

Finding Proof

The Web makes information so accessible that there is no excuse for not having proof. Just type some keywords into several different search engines and hit the Enter key. Proof can take many forms. Proof need not be absolute for everyone, but it must be absolutely convincing for your audience. Here are some sources:

→ *Newspaper articles.* If the point you're proving is newsworthy, document it with a newspaper or trade magazine article.

→ *Surveys.* Surveys and opinion polls are a great way to prove nebulous concepts like customer satisfaction, reader preference, brand perception, market acceptance, or product reliability over time. Often research companies in specific industries offer free research posted on their Web sites. You can also do your own surveys.

→ *Technical specs.* In technical fields, technical specifications can offer proof of claims.

→ *Anecdotal evidence.* Sometimes the most effective proof you can come up with is short stories of similar situations, where success was achieved in the market in which you are presenting. If you're presenting a new product to auto mechanics, having a few success stories of how auto mechanics in your area have used your solution can be the proof you need.

→ *Testimonials.* Sharing a series of letters from satisfied customers or organizations can often prove nebulous ideas like customer satisfaction or quality of service. After you have made a successful sale to an organization is a great time to ask them for a testimonial.

→ *Quote a recognized expert.* Also, quote from a well-respected Web site or book.

→ *Financial community reports.* Often the financial community publishes excellent reports on future trends. These are easy to find and authoritative to quote.

Dramatize Dull Key Facts

While selling magazine advertising space, I was handed a fact that should have given me a competitive advantage. My biggest competitor had dropped the independent audit of their circulation. Without an audit, a magazine publisher can easily misrepresent the magazine's circulation, and the claims of unaudited publications are often viewed with suspicion. But when I brought the dropped audit up to the next buying committee, it got little reaction.

Trying a different approach the following week in a presentation to a media board in Florida, I dramatized this dull fact. I began by saying, "I know that magazine audits are not the most interesting thing I can talk to you about (nods of agreement), but I wanted to show you just how important the auditing process can be."

My first slide was a newspaper article with a close-up on a headline that read,

Texas Board Investigating Andersen's Enron <u>Audit</u>

I had underlined the word *audit*. I began by talking dramatically about how it was the financial irregularities missed by Enron accounting audits that created the scandal that forced the Fortune 500 company into bankruptcy.

Then I said, "If you believe that ignoring audits can't cost you money..."

Here I cut to the next slide, an article with the headline

Enron <u>Audit</u> Costs Andersen Worldwide 60 Million

I continued: "Don't tell the people at Andersen Worldwide, Enron's auditors. They are losing a fortune from the fallout of the high profile scandal."

Finally I said, "Audits are so important that they can help decide the outcome of major elections. Everyone who lives in Florida should know this."

My next slide headline read

Judicial Watch <u>Audit</u> of Florida Presidential Ballots
Confirmed by Latest Media Recount... Independent
Audit Shows Bush Victory in Recount of Under Votes

The year was 2001 and Florida was still smarting from the sting of having the 2000 presidential election decided by the

Supreme Court after a huge legal battle over voter confusion. The idea that an audit helped pick the 43rd American president dramatized my point that audits can be dull but extremely important. With everyone's attention riveted on me, I moved into the not-as-exciting details of my magazine audits. Somehow they seemed more important that day.

Plan on Using a "Surprise" Fact

One way to get an audience involved quickly in your presentation is to start by stating a bold fact which forces them to react. For example, Mike Butts had just been promoted to marketing director for the Charlotte [North Carolina] Visitors' Association. Charlotte was a highly desirable destination for meetings and conventions, but there was no coordination among different community groups to present the city as an attractive destination to meeting planners. Butts intended to change that. He opened his first presentation before the Uptown General Managers Group with a slide that showed graphically the decline in state associations coming to Charlotte for their conventions. Then he stated his "surprise" fact: "The fact is that the state association market believes that Charlotte does not want their business—that *you* are not interested in their business anymore."

Some of the managers looked at Butts in surprise. He continued: "This may be hard for you to swallow, but how many of you have been to their trade shows lately, or how many of you have gone to Raleigh and made sales calls?" Then Butts laid out an action plan that got the general managers, and everyone else in Charlotte, involved in building Charlotte's association business up considerably.

Step by Step: Giving the Presentation

Play the Emotional Logic Card

The fact-based logical sell has tremendous emotional appeal. Surprise! This approach appeals to audiences who are smart and capable, or who just like being in control.

To appeal to this emotion, you must present yourself as a person willing to do a lot of extra homework to provide them with valuable information. You must be seen as a source of objective fact and information, not sales technique. You need to be viewed as a servant there to inform, not manipulate.

On some level, you are inviting the audience to be in control of the presentation. As you present every fact, they decide if they will accept or not accept what you tell them. The essence is, "I'll present the facts. You will decide based on the evidence. I won't insult your intelligence with a lot of emotional manipulation. You should only go along with this if it benefits your interests."

David Rosenberg, director of Strategic Accounts and Distribution at MacDermid Printing Solutions, is totally committed to fact-based selling. He explains his approach: "My own personal style is humility. I thank my audience for the opportunity to address them. I tell them that I realize their time is valuable and that I promise to leave them with items of real value as my way of saying "thank you" for allowing their time. This is an obligation I take very seriously as a professional in this industry, because I want to be invited back."

Present Your Facts

Your goal is to involve your audience in a process of discovery where they come to understand the importance of what you are proposing. As the logical case for your option unfolds, they're involved, in essence, in a step-by-step learning experience where they become convinced that your option represents the correct option.

Presenting each fact in your presentation is like a minipresentation in itself. You may start with a fact statement, then give an explanation as to why it is important, and follow with proof.

The power of sharing a series of facts is that they build on one another. In Princess Diana's presentation, accepting that landmines are a worldwide menace added weight to the next fact that Angola was so devastated by them. These two facts then added to the weight of the next that there is a false sense of economy supporting the use of landmines.

If your audience does not accept one of the facts in your sequence, you have to decide whether or not to keep on going. If it is a minor point that will not significantly affect the outcome, you can just minimize its impact by saying,

> Not all of us agree on this fact, but I hope as we continue you will reconsider.

or,

> Many of you may need more convincing on this point but there are more important facts to be shared. Let's put this point on hold and continue....

More often, I look forward to vigorous discussions at every point made. If there is no dialogue, controversy, or interaction, often there is no persuasion going on either.

Be the Sherlock Holmes of the Buying Decision

As you present your fact, be sensitive for clues that come up that reveal the decision-making process your audience is using.

Once while presenting to a buying committee that I expected to be unreceptive, I was surprised to discover significant differences of opinion among committee members. I paused my presentation and asked who agreed with what I had said so far. I was again surprised that everyone in the room agreed with my proposal except one very strong-willed individual who happened to control the budget. I suddenly realized that this "trail to the sale" had to cross this woman's desk! I put my prepared presentation aside, addressed her directly, and asked for her objections. For the next 15 minutes she and I were the only ones speaking in the room. Once she was sold, "as if by magic" everyone else in the audience was as well. As the great fictional detective Sherlock Holmes said, "It is of the highest importance in the art of detection to be able to recognize out of a number of facts which are incidental and which are vital."

Closing

The presentation that presents the facts is a step-by-step sequence of facts that impacts your audience's logical decision-making process. Closing a fact-based presentation is typically a summary of those facts, followed by a request for action.

David Rosenberg once closed a huge deal with an executive from one of the largest corporations in America. But there was a catch: He had to meet with this executive late in the evening in his downtown office. Rosenberg put his whole presentation on one sheet of paper. At the top it said, "Executive Summary." Below there were three points summarizing the benefits of his presentation:

1. Economic Impact
2. Quality Impact
3. Productivity Impact

Rosenberg assembled what he called "irrefutable and compelling evidence" below each of those bullets. The executive was very impressed with Rosenberg's summary, and Rosenberg closed his sale.

Cameron Bishop, president and CEO of Ascend Media, summed it up best when he said, "You start with your core point and then lead your audience down a logical path, supporting that path with the proper facts and figures to one ultimate conclusion."

8

The Presentation That Inspires

The mediocre teacher tells. The good teacher explains. The superior teacher demonstrates. The great teacher inspires. —William Arthur Ward (American educator, author, and pastor; 1921–1994)

If you want to build a ship, don't drum up people together to collect wood and don't assign them tasks and work, but rather teach them to long for the sea.—Antoine de Saint-Exupery (French writer and aviator; 1900–1944)

A check arrived at the Lee Iacocca Foundation from Mrs. Fox's fifth-grade class in Edgerton, Wisconsin. A note explained that the fifth graders had a classmate with diabetes and decided to contribute their holiday money to fight the disease.

A manila envelope arrived filled with a pile of checks from Shelby Sprung, a 13-year-old girl from New Jersey. An enclosed note explained that her sister had diabetes and that to celebrate Shelby's Bat Mitzvah, she had asked those sharing her special day to forgo writing the traditional check for herself and instead donate money to Iacocca's crusade against the disease.

San Diego's Rick Noble, whose daughter Kate was diagnosed with diabetes at the age of one, plans to raise money through Iacocca's campaign by attempting to climb Huayna Potasi, a 19,975-foot mountain in Bolivia.

The inspiration for these selfless acts began with Lee Iacocca, the legendary car man, whose wife, Mary, died of diabetes complications at age 57. Iacocca, now 80, is on the stump to fight the disease and to keep a promise.

His presentation begins: "I think about it every day. Twenty years ago, I promised my wife Mary that I would try to find a cure for diabetes in my lifetime. At the time, I was praying that a cure might happen in her lifetime, but as you know, we weren't that lucky. And I guess at 80 years old, you need to be realistic about how close you are to making that important promise I made come true."

Iacocca's promise to his wife strikes a deep chord in his audience. Like himself, most who attend his fundraisers have had loved ones hurt or killed by the disease. Then he shifts gears to describe the exciting work being done at Massachusetts General Hospital, led by Dr. Denise Faustman, whose research is funded by Iacocca's foundation. He tells the audience that Dr. Faustman has found a breakthrough treatment that, for the first time, has cured diabetes in mice. The audience breaks into spontaneous applause at the news.

"Don't applaud," quips Iacocca. "As I like to say, if you're a mouse... I think I've got you covered.... But you're not a mouse." The audience laughs appreciatively but understands Iacocca's deeper message: This is hopeful news, but not a cure. Iacocca continues to describe the research and the long road it took to get to this point. He talks about how funds are needed to move this theoretical finding out of the lab and "into the real world of human clinical trials."

Iacocca concludes: "I hope that I'm here with you 10 years from now. All of you, starting with myself [applause]. So that we can come back and celebrate our success together. Now, if I'm not around [voice heavy with emotion], I'd like to know that I've created an organization that would carry on and fulfill the promise that I made to my wife. Simply stated, I'm asking everyone here tonight to become my partner in this journey."

After I interviewed Lee Iacocca and heard these stories I visited his Web site, www.joinleenow.com, and made my own donation. It was impossible not to.

HOW THIS WORKS

Every person on earth desperately needs to know that his or her life is more than just the sum of its daily routines. The presentation that inspires presents an action that, if taken, will connect the audience to something extremely great or meaningful.

Pitfalls

Thinking You Can Inspire a Hostile Audience

The presentation that inspires works bests for audiences that are already on your side. This presentation moves people from acceptance to belief and action. If you are encountering audience skepticism from the start, I recommend trying a different approach, at least initially.

Thinking You Have to Be a Gifted Genius, a Sainted Visionary, or Touched by a Greater Spiritual Force to Inspire an Audience

While it is true that many visionaries are geniuses, more often I find that true geniuses have trouble articulating any vision, as well as simple driving instructions. Men and women of ordinary intelligence and ability routinely construct and share inspirational messages, provided they have the heart, true belief, and willingness to work hard. However, the presenter who inspires an audience for the first time does need to learn a new communication skill and put in the effort. The "gift" of inspiration is 90 percent perspiration.

Thinking That the "Vision" Comes to Leaders in a Blinding Flash as They Step in Front of an Audience

Such a vision does not come in a flash, according to Carolyn Archambault, director of Entertainment Technology Division at Wall Street Communications. She has seen many inspirational CEOs who work hard on their vision message. According to Archambault, the best CEOs customize their vision message for different audiences, evolve it with changing times, and seek constant feedback so they can keep improving it. When they take to a podium, their vision message may seem spontaneous, but it is actually well practiced and carefully thought through.

Step by Step: Preparation

Create a Vision

The basic message of an inspirational presentation is, "Do this [donate to diabetes research, work hard to beat a competitor, vote for John Doe, join a gym, etc.] and you will be part of something bigger, more important, and truly meaningful." But what does your audience need to be a part of? Finding a vision that describes this desirable place is the most critical part of the process. If your vision is on target, you almost certainly will win, as audiences will forgive almost anything else if you show them a vision that moves them. But if your vision is off target, you will almost certainly fail.

Your vision needs to be clear, real, and pragmatic so that your audience can grasp its full meaning and visualize it in their minds. Once created, this vision becomes the magnet that pulls your audience over unanticipated obstacles as they work hard to attain it. What follow are a number of time-tested approaches to help find that inspirational vision.

Ask, "Deep in Their Hearts, What Does My Audience Need or Want to Believe?"

Sometimes finding an inspirational vision becomes obvious if you take the time to understand the yearnings, hopes, and dreams of your audience.

Alan Gerson is the 9/11 city councilman of New York City. It was in his district, District 1, where the World Trade Center once stood. In the months after the Twin Towers were attacked, Gerson was a constant presence in his district, inspiring his constituents to keep their spirits up and hopes alive. It did not take long for him to understand the kind of inspiring vision they needed to hear.

Gerson recalls: "In the aftermath of the crisis, people were looking to have their underlying hope and optimism reaffirmed. I would point out the goodness that was surrounding us. I would say, 'What is even more significant than 9/11 is 9/12, the day after, when we realized the depth of goodness and compassion that maybe we didn't know was there. We have people helping people, neighbor helping neighbor, stranger helping stranger. We have become a more complete community.'" Gerson's inspiring words continue to keep the spirit of District 1 alive today.

Look for Greatness in Small, Everyday Events

History records that the American civil rights movement began on December 1, 1955, when Rosa Parks, a seamstress in Montgomery, Alabama, was arrested for refusing to give up her seat to a white man on a crowded city bus. But the "Jim Crow" laws that supported her arrest had been in place for years, not just in Montgomery, but all over the southern United States. Yet, through the eyes of the new pastor at the Dexter Avenue Baptist Church, this was not just a routine incident, but a call to destiny. In his autobiography, Martin Luther King, Jr. called the speech he was about to give about Mrs. Parks's arrest "the most decisive speech of my life." In the book, *The Preacher King,* author Richard Lescher describes:

From the beginning of his public career King sought to elevate local battles into holy Crusades of mythic proportions. In his address at the Holt Street Church he skillfully elevated the significance of Rosa Parks's arrest from an all-too-familiar ugly incident to the test of an entire people's resolve to claim its own dignity.

King's words inspired the audience to see the historic greatness of the moment. The civil rights movement had begun. Lee Iacocca did the same thing when he invited his audience to be a part of history at a possible turning point in the battle against a terrible disease.

Take a Step Back

Sometimes you can find a vision by pulling back for a look at the larger view of your product or option's global effect. In other words, don't talk about how your product will benefit your customers, talk about how it will set things in motion that will change the world. Don't talk about how your service will make their lives better, talk about how the values found in your service have the potential to make *everyone's* lives better.

To give this approach a try, fill in the blanks:

We're not just _____. We are_____!

Here's how Steven Jobs used this approach in 1984, as he introduced the Macintosh, the first cost-effective personal computer with a graphical user interface:

We're not just... introducing a computer with a new graphical interface.

We are... unveiling a computer that will change the
world. The Macintosh is "the computer for the rest of
us." Because of its graphical interface, anyone, not just
large corporations and government, can now operate a
computer!

At a trade show press presentation I saw Michel Proulx, vice
president of Product Development at Miranda Technologies, introduce an innovative video decoder that would enable low-cost video
cameras to output broadcast quality signals. In essence he said:

We're not just... introducing a video decoder that out-
puts high-quality video signals from low-cost cameras.

We are... introducing a product that will democratize
video. Suddenly anyone, on any budget, can create video
that will be capable of communicating their message with
broadcast quality images!

A vision is rarely about a specific product, candidate, or proposal. More often it champions an entire category of products,
or even humanity itself.

Share a Perspective That Connects to a Bigger Picture

To inspire some of the workers in his factory, David Ross, president of Ross Video Ltd., shared a vision of two workers laboring
in the Middle Ages, both sitting in front of a pile of rocks:

You ask the first guy what he's doing and he says, "My
job is to pick up this rock and bash it on all six sides
until it's roughly the shape of a brick. Then I put it in

that pile over there and I get another rock, bash it until all the sides are flat and put that in the pile too."

You ask him, "How do you feel about your job?" and he says, "I hate it. It's boring and I will be doing this the rest of my life."

You turn to the guy right beside him, who's doing exactly the same thing, and you ask him what he is doing. He says: "I'm building a glorious cathedral. And I'm devoting my life to it and it's going to stand for a thousand years. I feel privileged." You ask how he feels about his job and he says he loves it and feels lucky to have it.

After that, Ross explains to his factory workers how every job, no matter how small, is connected to an important result. Ross concludes his presentations: "There are two ways to look at your job. Which are you doing? Are you selecting resistors out of a bin and plugging them in, or are you part of the entertainment industry? Are you working a day-to-day job or are you building the technology that makes the next Madonna concert possible? We have stuff that's going up in the space station. You have the coolest job within a thousand miles of here."

Oliver Wendell Holmes said, "Man's mind, stretched by a new idea, never goes back to its original dimensions."

Target a Competitor

If your audience faces significant competition, inspiration can come from a vision that helps them overcome that competitor. It's like the locker room talk a coach gives the team before they head out to the playing field.

While describing his formula for "everyday evangelism" in his book *Selling the Dream*, Guy Kawasaki wrote, "Enemies are optional, but they are a desirable element because they provide a focal point for a cause. Perhaps it's human nature but it's often more fun to *defeat* bad than to *do* good."

The rallying cry to beat an evil competitor can be a great inspiration.

Help People

In the 1970s, Bob Lipp, now president of The Marcomm Group, was asked to promote a bodybuilding event. Back then, bodybuilders were viewed as oddballs. To promote this event, Lipp organized a series of events at local schools and hotels where speakers would talk about, not bodybuilding, but health and fitness.

The talks were designed to inspire people to develop healthy lifestyles and encourage support of regular exercise, of which bodybuilding was one of many covered. As speakers, Lipp used local people who had achieved success in each area. As the audiences heard the stories, many became inspired to explore new avenues, among them bodybuilding, to achieve a healthier lifestyle.

When the bodybuilding event came to town, hundreds of people who previously had never even heard of bodybuilding packed the hall.

Ask yourself, is there an aspect of your product or option that can help people in a broader way? Focusing on the broader message of self-improvement or helping those in need can inspire in ways that focusing on a specific product or option will not.

Step by Step: Giving the Presentation

To Give an Inspiring Presentation, You Need an Inspiring Buildup and Introduction

As the messenger of an important vision, it helps if you start off, ever so slightly, on a pedestal. You are asking your audience to believe in a vision they cannot see or touch. Before they believe in your vision they have to believe in you. You must be introduced as being far more than merely competent, you must be seen as a thought leader in their space. An audience who *expects* to see an inspiring speaker is much more likely to see one.

Modesty aside, I am frequently hired to inspire salespeople. Before the presentation, I work with the clients who have hired me to prepare the audience. Typically they buy copies of my books that I autograph for audience members, distribute articles I have written, and introduce me with strong reference to my books, international book translations, and appearances on national television. By the time I show up, my audience is ready to hear someone they can believe in.

But I was once hired to speak to the sales staff of a newly acquired company, by the acquiring organization. The sales director who managed the staff was not enthusiastic that I was coming. He saw me as a messenger and spy for the new owners. He ordered no books, and at five minutes before showtime asked me, "Hey Josh, something just came up, would you mind introducing yourself?" During my presentation he sat in the back whispering among a group of his associates, and during an interactive exercise I discovered that his group was doing the opposite of what I had asked.

My presentation went okay, but it did not inspire the way it usually does. It is much harder to inspire an audience when you start with a completely "cold" room. There is a reason that rock bands and comedians have warm-up acts before they come on stage. Expectation is a tremendously powerful part of giving a presentation that inspires. To inspire an audience, make sure you arrange for an inspiring lead-in and introduction.

Start with an Audience but Build a Congregation

The moment you make a vision stick there is a collective "ah-ha" that ripples through the audience. As a presenter, there are few greater feelings than seeing this magical moment. But I am mindful that the magic does not come from the podium but from the audience itself. When a room full of people "get it" all at the same time, inspiration begets inspiration, and the collective feeling of all audience members comes together to create a larger persuasive event. Since reaching this point is your goal, you need *all* of your audience along for the ride.

Every audience has several smaller audiences within it. They can be divided by many criteria such as age, level of experience, or interest. I was once invited to speak at a magazine publishing convention to an audience of advertising space salespeople about selling ad space. What I did not know was that the trade show associated with the conference shut down during the presentations, and that a large group of exhibitors with nothing else to do had opted to join my session. I suddenly realized that I was presenting to an audience of 75 percent advertising space salespeople, along with about 25 percent salespeople from printing companies.

But like a good pastor leading a congregation, I knew that I could leave no one behind.

Instead of saying, "when selling magazine ad space," I shifted to say, "when selling magazine ad space or printing services."

After illustrating a point with an example from the world of magazine ad space sales, I called on a printing salesperson who helped me with an example from his world. I looked for every opportunity to make the printing salespeople feel every bit as important as my main audience.

Let Them Know Who You Are

When Carolyn Archambault, director of Entertainment Technology at Wall Street Communications, works with CEOs to deliver inspirational messages, she coaches them to let their personalities show. Archambault believes that when a CEO shares a vision, he or she is as much a part of the vision as the vision itself.

If an audience does not believe in or understand the presenter, they will not believe in the vision. People will take a leap of faith with a speaker they believe in. Sometimes a vision is more about who has created it and is sharing it than about the vision itself.

Lee Iacocca showed a very personal side of himself when he shared the story of the promise he made to his wife. After hearing that story, no audience member could doubt his sincerity.

An Ounce of Doubt Will Kill You

In the presentation that inspires, you are asking your audience to take a leap to a place in the future they cannot touch, see, or smell. Your audience has to have total faith in you, and in what you are advocating.

With some other types of presentations I suggest that offering an "objective" view of your competition can help win credibility, but not here. With the presentation that inspires, you need to believe so completely that if asked about competition you reply, "We have none. This is the only way."

Add Examples

I often find that the point at which an audience "gets it" is when you apply what you describe in the big picture to a practical example specific to their world. While presenting to the marketing staff of a midsize company that favored a very traditional approach, I encouraged them to take a bold leap and embrace a new set of electronic marketing tools. I described the revolution in marketing sweeping the globe, the emerging power of the Internet, and shared success stories.

But my dramatics about the future were cut short when an impatient sounding data entry person asked a question: "This is all very exciting, Josh, but how would we add new names to our existing customer mailing list?" I explained a variety of ways the new technologies could link to their lists. As I explained this small detail I saw the light go on in their minds. After they got the bit about the mailing lists, the rest of the "great sweeping changes of global marketing" began to make sense as well.

To make a vision stick your audience needs to see that it connects to their world on a granular level. Sometimes a dialogue about the practical applications can help make a "big picture" vision real and a leap of faith safe.

Explain the Big Picture in Practical Terms

Sometimes the way to make a vision stick is to offer an extremely practical side and make it understandable. Perhaps the most inspirational speech of this kind was given in 1963 by John F. Kennedy in an address at the American University on the subject of "peace." At the time, *peace* was not a word found in many newspapers; the Cold War was in full force, the memory of the superpowers at the brink of nuclear war over the Cuban missile crisis was still fresh, and there was widespread pessimism as a nuclear arms race and hostile rhetoric were escalating.

In his address, Kennedy projected optimism about the human spirit and took direct aim at the pessimists who doubted the possibility of a lasting peace:

> Too many of us think it is impossible. Too many think it unreal. But that is a dangerous, defeatist belief. It leads to the conclusion that war is inevitable—that mankind is doomed—that forces grip us we cannot control.
>
> We need not accept that view. Our problems are manmade—therefore, man can solve them. And man can be as big as he wants. No problem of human destiny is beyond human beings. Man's reason and spirit have often solved the seemingly unsolvable—and we believe they can do it again.

Then Kennedy shared his vision of world peace in extremely practical terms:

> Genuine peace must be the product of many nations, the sum of many acts.... For peace is a process—a way of solving problems.
>
> With such a peace, there will still be quarrels and conflicting interests, as there are within families and nations. World peace, like community peace, does not require that each man love his neighbor—it requires only that they live together in mutual tolerance, submitting their disputes to a just and peaceful settlement....
>
> So let us persevere. Peace need not be impracticable, and war need not be inevitable. By defining our goal

more clearly, by making it seem more manageable and less remote, we can help all peoples to see it, to draw hope from it, and to move irresistibly toward it.

Kennedy went on the talk about the common interest in peace that both the American and Soviet people shared and vowed that the United States would not test another nuclear weapon unless another nation did so first. The speech was downplayed by the American press and largely forgotten after a civil rights address by Kennedy the following evening.

But Kennedy's speech had huge impact in Moscow. Soviet Premier Khrushchev would later call it, "the best speech by any president since Roosevelt." And the Soviet press published the full text of the speech.

More importantly, the speech broke through an electronic barrier that had been in place since the start of the Cold War. Just after World War II, the U.S. government began sending its Voice of America radio broadcast into the Soviet Union to offer an alternative point of view. In response, the Soviet Union had built a network of 3,000 transmitters to jam those broadcasts across the full breadth of the Soviet Union. But the day a Russian translation of Kennedy's speech was transmitted over the Voice of America, those 3,000 transmitters mysteriously shut down, letting all but one paragraph especially critical of the Soviets be relayed directly to the people of the Soviet Union. And when the Voice of America rebroadcast the speech, it was not jammed at all. Then, suddenly, the Soviets stopped jamming all Western broadcasts.

An inspiring message of peace, with a very practical side, had freed up communication and lessened the likelihood that the Cold War would become a nuclear war.

Closing

If Your Vision Sticks, Then It Is Time for a Call to Action

The close can be straightforward. Simply tell your audience that if they believe then they should act. A classic way to do this is to tell your audience that they are at a crossroads of destiny and ask which way they want to go.

When John Sculley, then-president of PepsiCo, turned down Steven Jobs's offer to run Apple Computer, Jobs regrouped and asked Sculley a question that forced him to reconsider. Recalled Sculley in his book, *Odyssey: Pepsi to Apple:*

> After a weighty, uncomfortable pause, he [Jobs] issued a challenge that would haunt me for days: "Do you want to spend the rest of your life selling sugared water or do you want a chance to change the world?"
>
> It was as if someone reached up and delivered a stiff blow to my stomach. I had been worried about giving up my future at Pepsi.... Steve was telling me my entire life was at a critical crossroads. The question was a monstrous one; one for which I had no answer. It simply knocked the wind out of me.

The presentation that inspires asks an audience to take a leap of faith and take an action to join something bigger and more important. John Sculley did just this, as he reacted to Jobs's question and joined Apple Computer as CEO in 1983.

9

The Presentation That Changes a Perception

All our knowledge has its origins in our perceptions.—Leonardo da Vinci (Italian painter, sculptor, architect, engineer; 1452–1519)

To effectively communicate, we must realize that we are all different in the way we perceive the world and use this understanding as a guide to our communication with others.—Tony Robbins (American motivational speaker & writer; 1960–)

In the animal kingdom, the rule is, eat or be eaten; in the human kingdom, define or be defined.—Thomas Szasz (U.S. psychiatrist, educator; 1920–)

If you want to make enemies, try to change something.—Woodrow Wilson (U.S. president; 1913–1921)

In early 1993 international pressure intensified on the all-white government of South Africa to hold elections that would include the majority black population. But negotiations with Nelson Mandela's African National Congress (ANC) party about the elections had dragged to a standstill.

The South African government, after centuries of repressive tactics, feared vengeful acts if a black majority government took power. Mandela was convinced that the long and hard negotiations had failed and that a date for elections would never be set. As the stand-off continued and tensions mounted, a shocking event occurred that threatened to launch the nation into a race-based civil war.

On April 10, Chris Hani, second in command at the ANC party behind only Mandela himself, was brutally assassinated by a white militant. Hani's strongest supporters were the ANC's young black militants who could easily have taken his murder as a cry for all-out war.

With civil war a very real threat, the current government encouraged Mandela to address the nation to calm the crisis. Mandela's appearance on national television may have surprised many, as only three years before he had been released from a South African jail where he had spent the past 27 years.

Mandela's immediate task was to change the perception that Hani's murder was a repressive act plotted by the South African government and which demanded swift and bloody revenge. He needed to replace this with the perception that this tragedy actually presented an opportunity for positive change. His nationally televised address was repeated three times the day before Hani's funeral.

Mandela's heartfelt first sentence made it clear he was speaking to the entire country: "Tonight I am reaching out to every single South African, black and white, from the very depths of my being." Then Mandela emphasized that Hani's murder was

not a repressive act by the South African government, but instead
by a hateful man whose horrible crime should unite all South
Africans:

> A white man, full of prejudice and hate, came to our
> country and committed a deed so foul that our whole
> nation now teeters on the brink of disaster. A white
> woman, of Afrikaner origin, risked her life so that we
> may know, and bring to justice, this assassin.... What has
> happened is a national tragedy that has touched millions
> of people, across the political and colour divide.

Mandela then asked white South Africans to share in the
mourning of a national hero at Hani's funeral the next day. He
described Hani as a man of peace who would not have wanted
his death to spark violence that could derail the negotiations
toward open elections.

Mandela concluded, "Our decision and actions will determine
whether we use our pain, our grief, and outrage to move forward
to what is the only lasting solution for our country—an elected
government of the people, by the people, and for the people."

Mandela kept the peace by changing the perception of what
this tragedy meant for his country. For him, the benefits of
redefining this tragedy had very real results. White South Africans
took notice that it was Mandela's calming voice, not a voice from
the current government, which kept the peace. Behind the scenes,
Mandela's handling of the crisis so increased his stature that when
he returned to the negotiating table with the South African government, his demand to set an election date could not be denied.
Three months later in July, history was made when the all-white
government of South Africa agreed to hold open elections that
would inevitably shift power to the black majority.

HOW THIS WORKS

If your audience has a negative attitude toward an aspect of your proposal, it will be hard to win approval. But trying to change a deep-rooted attitude often triggers a negative reaction.

Luckily for the persuasive presenter, there is a "back door" to the human mind. Every attitude is formed from the initial perceptions that created it. Change those perceptions and you can change the attitude. Change the attitude and new behavior will follow.

Pitfalls

Assuming Your Audience Has No Preconceived Notions

There is a vast amount of new information about businesses and organizations available today within easy access. You must assume that every audience you address has some initial perceptions about you, your organization, your product or idea category, and perhaps even your proposal before you arrive. The perceptions they bring into the room will affect the outcome of your presentation.

Directly Challenging an Audience to Change an Attitude

Unless you have some direct control over an audience, telling them they should "change their attitude" rarely works. In fact, this approach usually causes a defensive reaction among your audience members that reinforces the very attitude you are trying to change. John Kenneth Galbraith, the great economist, wrote, "Faced with the choice between changing one's mind and proving there is no need to do so, almost everyone gets busy on the proof."

Step by Step: Preparation

Ask Yourself, "What Attitude Needs to Change?"

If your audience is not already supporting your proposal, they have an attitude about some aspect of it that is either not completely positive or is unresolved. The attitude might not be negative and could simply be a case of needing clarification. Or, there could be a perception lodged in their collective minds from a previous experience, news item, hearsay, or malicious bad-mouthing from a competitor that needs to be vetted and changed.

To plan for this presentation, you need to anticipate what attitudes may be standing in the way of the audience buying your proposal. I find that while you cannot always predict the specific attitude that eventually becomes your target, the process of thinking through all the different possibilities is the best preparation for whatever you encounter.

Here is an exercise to help anticipate what attitudes may need adjusting. Just fill in the blanks:

If my audience had a different attitude toward _____

_____,

they would [write your goal here] _____

_____.

Ask Yourself, "What Are the Underlying Perceptions behind Their Attitude?"

I once proposed producing a training video that used puppets to help illustrate key points. I was surprised when several people in my corporate audience immediately reacted negatively. When I asked why, I was told that two years earlier, another training producer had created a puppet video for them that was terrible. The burly vice president of human resources stood, and with a reddening face snarled at me, "Listen, I'm only going to tell you this once. From corporate headquarters on down, we despise puppets!"

The attitude that even good puppets make bad training videos came from perceptions formulated during that earlier bad experience. Arguing general puppet virtue would never change the attitude of this hardened lot. To win the day I asked to go back and discuss the time when their first negative perceptions about puppets were formulated. After they were vetted, I went on to show how my proposal was different from that of the earlier producer, and how my skills and approach would have a very different result. The puppet proposal became a serious contender.

Offer Something New That Displaces or Changes the Original Perception

Changing a perception is a creative process by which you introduce a more compelling perception to displace the existing one. Here are some approaches to consider.

Offer a New Way to Look at Things. In the summer of 1976 as a camp counselor I faced my toughest audience ever: 60 tired and hungry seven-year-old hikers. We had just broken for lunch when my junior counselor rushed up to me panic-struck. Through a mix-up in the kitchen, a third of our group's peanut butter and jelly sandwiches were made from the end pieces from loaves of bread. We were deep in a New England forest and days from the nearest McDonald's, and the sandwiches were all we had to offer. A quick crisis assessment told me that 20 kids were going to have to eat sandwiches made with bread loaf ends and half would be crying within a minute after I announced this.

As I held one of the undesirable sandwiches in my hand I noticed that, from a side view, the sandwich made with the ends curved to a point like the front of a rocket ship. Seizing on this I told the junior counselor to put the "end" sandwiches at the far side of the picnic table. Holding an "end" sandwich high above my head I announced in a loud, clear voice, "I have good news and bad news. The good news is that we have something completely new here at camp today, an aerodynamically sound peanut butter and jelly sandwich." I "zoomed" the sandwich through the air to demonstrate how the tapered point offered much less wind resistance than your ordinary, boring peanut butter and jelly sandwich. Then I announced the bad news that we had only 20 of them, so not everyone would get one for lunch that day.

One boy in the front noticed that the aerodynamic sandwiches were piled at the end of the table farthest from him. As he made a desperate lunge for one of the sandwiches, a stampede of seven-year-olds followed.

The aftermath of the sandwich-grabbing frenzy left one girl crying because her hand was stepped on in the stampede and two boys who would only stop crying when promised extra "aerodynamically sound" sandwiches when we returned to base camp.

Here is a seven-year-old's perception of the sandwiches before my demonstration: "Sandwiches made with the two ends of a loaf of bread are yucky."

Here is a seven-year-old's perception of the sandwiches after my demonstration: "Sandwiches made with two ends offer much less wind resistance than ordinary, boring sandwiches. Cool!"

Redefine the Process of Evaluation. At the 1952 Republican National Convention, then-Senator Richard Nixon was nominated to become Dwight D. Eisenhower's vice-presidential running mate. Shortly afterward, Eisenhower was surprised when the *New York Post* exposed a secret campaign fund Nixon had been keeping, by publishing the headline, "Secret Rich Men's Trust Fund Keeps Nixon in Style Far Beyond His Salary." Some Democrats began asking whether Nixon could be trusted with the nation's finances when his own were being managed questionably, and they demanded that Nixon withdraw his candidacy.

Nixon vowed full disclosure, and Eisenhower withheld judgment as to whether to keep him on the presidential ticket until afterward. Nixon presented his case to a national television audience. As he started his address Nixon did not deny accepting the money, but he did redefine the question of how he should be evaluated. Said Nixon, "The legal issue is not enough. The real question is one of morality." Then, Nixon defined how that moral question should be judged: "I say that it was morally wrong if any of that $18,000 went to Senator Nixon for my personal use. I say it was morally wrong if it was secretly given and secretly handled. And I say that it was morally wrong if any of the contributors got special favors for the contributions that they made."

Then, he went on to explain that he did not personally benefit from the fund and that the fund was actually not nearly as secret as the newspaper reports would have everyone believe. Nixon then went on to claim that no contributor to the fund received, "any consideration that he would not have received as an ordinary constituent."

Nixon then used a chronological description of his personal finances to take his audience on a tour of his admirable life story: how, from humble beginnings full of struggle and grit, he had achieved his present-day success.

Nixon closed on a personal note by describing one additional unreported campaign gift he had accepted—this one completely without remorse. A supporter from Texas had, after hearing Nixon mention that his "two youngsters" wanted a dog, taken the initiative and sent him one. When the dog arrived, Nixon's six-year-old daughter, Tricia, named it Checkers. Nixon concluded, "The kids, like all kids, loved the dog, and regardless of what they say about it, we're going to keep it."

Americans widely accepted Nixon's explanation in what became known as his "Checkers speech," and Eisenhower kept him on the presidential ticket.

Perception of Nixon before the speech: "Uncertain. Inappropriate accounting can be a sign of dishonesty."

Perception of Nixon after the speech: "Not a great bookkeeper, but an American who worked his way up the hard way and who deserves the benefit of the doubt."

Assign Different Attributes. The first night of Girl Scout camp was sleepless, thanks to the heat, humidity, and bugs. The bugs, inch-long, black, June bugs, were the biggest offenders as they became attracted to the girls' cabin lights and slammed themselves repeatedly against the screen doors. As I stopped by to wish my 11-year-old daughter, Jenny, a good night, I found her wide awake and anxiously huddled on a bunk bed with a friend. I could hear the sound of several June bugs banging noisily against their cabin door, while an especially large June bug casually climbed the wall facing them.

"Are the June bugs scaring you?" I asked.

Two heads nodded anxiously.

As I looked at the large bug climbing the facing wall, an idea to diffuse their fears came to me. From my college years as an entomology major, I recalled that many climbing insects will display a survival reflex when threatened and suddenly drop to the ground to escape danger.

I began, "The thing you don't realize is that the June bugs are not hitting against your cabin door because they want to get in to hurt you, they are attracted to the light and just don't know any better. Do you know the real reason they're banging against your cabin door?"

The two shook their heads.

I exclaimed loudly, "It's because they're stupid."

The two huddled campers looked surprised.

"I'm going to show you just how dumb these bugs are," I told them.

I stepped over to the June bug climbing the wall in front of them. I cupped a hand about a foot below the bug and inched a finger toward its head.

"Watch this. He thinks he's going to escape from me but he's so dumb, he's going to jump right into my hand!"

As my finger came within a quarter inch of the bug's head the survival reflex kicked in and the bug dropped into my hand with a big plunk!

The 11-year-olds cheered and laughed. They excitedly exclaimed, "He's not so scary, he's just stupid!" The June bugs just didn't seem so bothersome after that.

Eleven-year-old perception of June bugs before my demonstration: "They are big, black, and trying to bang their way into our cabin to 'get us.' Scary!"

Eleven-year-old perception of June bugs after my demonstration: "Not scary, just really stupid."

Share a New "Standard." As Nigel Spratling, marketing vice president of a technology company, looked ahead toward a major industry trade show, he feared no one would visit his booth. Through a series of delays there would be no new products at his booth this year to attract visitors. As it turned out, though, Spratling's booth went on to become one of the hottest booths at the show despite the lack of new products.

Spratling realized that there was a real industry problem in interfacing technical products from different manufacturers. Acting on his own, he shaped a collection of best-practice measurements into a set of "standards" that would assure good product interfacing. Spratling called it PIS, the Precision Interface Standard.

He had his company's products independently tested to prove they were compliant with these "standards," and wrote a white paper on the need for a PIS which was published in industry trade publications prior to the show. Finally, he printed "PIS compliant" stickers and pasted them on his company's products, and then he ran ads in industry trade magazines announcing that his products were "PIS compliant."

As word spread about this new, extremely useful "standard," crowds flocked to Spratling's booth. Many of his competitors were caught completely off guard when visitors entering their booths challenged them to produce proof that their products were also PIS compliant.

Perception of Spratling's trade show booth before PIS: "No new products, no need to visit."

Perception of Spratling's booth after PIS: "An industry leader where new standards are being set. If we can visit only one booth at the show this is it!"

Share Positive Stories of Change. Dawn Brown, president of Perception Shift and author of *That Perception Thing*, started out as a psychologist who noticed the empowering benefit of having her clients shift their own perceptions. When her clients would find themselves locked into a painful pattern, she would show them how to recognize their own power to move past the pain by shifting their perceptions.

A few years ago Brown was asked to speak to help resolve a bitter labor-management dispute. Her event was staged to promote social involvement between the two groups, so every table had management and union people seated together.

Recalled Brown, "I felt it was important to be subtle. I knew they had big problems so I didn't make overt reference to them. Instead I shared examples of problem situations where people had thought they couldn't forgive each other and move past painful situations, but did so, not by getting the other party to change, but by changing their own perception of the other party first."

Concludes Brown, "We want others to change. But our point of power is ourselves and our ability to change our own perceptions." As dinner continued, the attitude improved. Shortly afterward, the labor-management dispute was settled amicably.

Management and union perception of each other before Brown's dinner: "%*&#@!$X#!!!"

Management and union perception of each other after Brown's dinner: "We may have disagreement, but if we change our perceptions of each other we can both benefit."

Redefine a Perception by Adding Fun. Every day at Audubon Nature Camp, Rick Cowley the geology counselor, and I, the entomology counselor, faced a huge challenge at morning assembly. We, and a half-dozen other specialized science counselors, would stand in front of all the six-to-twelve-year-old campers and give a summary of the morning activity session we would be offering in our specialty. The Audubon Society is world famous for its bird-watching enthusiasts, so the bird counselor always got the biggest play. When your session was about rocks or bugs it was hard to compete with the plant, reptile, mammal, craft, and photography counselors.

Rick and I would watch helplessly each morning as dozens of campers would head out birding or to a photography session, while only a handful of campers would come to ours. One morning though, Rick prepared a presentation that would forever change the perception of the "rock class" at Audubon Camp.

Without fanfare, Rick stood and announced: "There will be a rock feeding at the Geology Hut at the start of our morning session." A stunned looking eight-year-old piped up in the front row, "Hey, everyone knows you can't feed rocks." Not missing a beat, Rick pulled out a football-sized piece of pumice, an extremely porous volcanic rock. He said, "Just as baby birds need care and feeding, so do the rock specimens at the Geology Hut." Without explanation, Rich zipped out a water bottle and squirted the rock.

To the delight of the campers, the pumice soaked up every drop of squirted water. Rick mugged to his audience and exclaimed, "Boy, I didn't realize he was so thirsty." The campers erupted into spontaneous applause. Rick continued, "If you want to see him get a real meal, come to the geology session this morning." That morning Audubon camp history was made as more campers went to see Rick's rocks than went birding.

Perception of Rick's morning geology session before his demonstration: "Rocks are boring."

Perception of Rick's morning geology session after his demonstration: "Rick's rocks rock!"

Step by Step: Giving the Presentation

Give Your Audience Permission to Change

Peer pressure among audience members to keep the status quo can be a powerful deterrent to change. To diffuse this, start with a short, face-saving statement to support those open to change. With some highly political audiences to whom I have presented, nothing would have happened had I not done this.

Your short, pro-change statement takes the negative judgment out of the room and makes it okay to consider change. Here are some approaches.

That Was Then, This Is Now. Point out a trend, new technology, news event, or pivotal situation that redefines the situation. It is okay to consider change, because something about the situation has changed. For example:

→ "In light of the rise in interest rates, everyone needs to reevaluate their financial investments. Here is an option you may not have considered…"

→ "The Internet has put new information into the hands of your customers. As a result, it is important to consider this when you reconsider any IT system."

→ "After 9-11 we all need to reexamine our security needs. Here are some aspects of your current security system you may not have considered…"

"It's My Fault." If your offering is so terrific, why isn't your audience using it already? The better your proposal starts to sound, the dumber your audience may look for their past judgment.

Claiming this missed opportunity was your fault takes the burden off your audience because

→ You failed to contact their organization in a timely fashion.
→ You failed to show them the benefits clearly.
→ You didn't understand their needs.

This Is Completely Different. By pointing out how your offering is very different from past offerings, you give your audience permission to reconsider something they had rejected in the past.

Seek Confirmation

After you share your face-saving statement, ask your audience for confirmation that they accept your statement that change is okay. Say something like, "I hope we can all agree that with this trend, evaluating new options becomes important." Then, look carefully at the audience. If you see nods of agreement, then proceed. If you get no reaction from your audience, follow up on this. Say, "Is this okay with everyone?" or "You do agree with what I'm saying, don't you?" Most often they will give you an okay and you can proceed.

But I have had presentations where at this point someone says, "I don't agree with you at all. We have no reason to change." If you ask, "Why not?" you will often end up addressing a concern you did not anticipate, but that needs addressing.

Confirm Your Target Attitude

After giving the audience permission to change, I proceed to confirm that the attitude I anticipated to be the one needing change is in fact the one I need to change. I typically ask for confirma-

tion of my assumptions with a simple question. For instance, if
the attitude I have anticipated is that my audience thinks my
solution is too expensive, I might say:

"Before I begin, let me ask you a question. How many in this
audience believe that my solution is one you can't afford? Could
I see a show of hands?"

If the attitude I have anticipated is that my audience thinks that
adapting to a new technology is not worth the effort, I might say:

"A recent survey showed that only about 15 percent of all television studios have actually moved from analog to digital technology. How many in this room still have analog plants? How
many would make the change if they could?"

Assuming you get confirmation that you have correctly identified the attitudes that need to change, proceed with the
approach you've prepared. If not, perhaps a dialogue will result
that will take you to a different point of discussion.

As You Work the Room, Ask Yourself, "Who Owns the Decision I'm Trying to Change?"

Every audience has a hierarchy to it, and within that hierarchy are
some individuals who are more important in the decision-making
process than others. For example, there are thought leaders, people whom others in the audience respect either through position,
expertise, or accomplishment. If you can identify these thought
leaders in your audience and play a bit more to them, very often
their conversion can help you sway the rest of the audience.

If you are presenting to a buying committee, very often there
is a corporate structure within your audience where specific individuals have far more control over the decision than others. Make
sure you identify and play to these individuals.

I often find that within an audience, the people who speak up to ask questions, voice concerns, or share stories are motivated to do so politically. They may be trying to assert their existing corporate authority, or they may be attempting to exert authority they believe they have because of their unique expertise. Be sensitive to the people who share in your audience and try to understand who influences what in terms of the ultimate decisions your audience will make. Sometimes in an audience there are only a handful of people who actually make the decision you are trying to influence. The nature of the questions people ask often reveal their political stature within the organization.

Closing

This chapter began with the idea that perceptions drive attitudes and attitudes drive behavior. To close, we simply follow the same pattern in reverse.

First confirm that the perception you have sought to change has, in fact, changed. Ask the audience, "Does anyone still believe that Smith Street is as dangerous as it was back in the 1980s, or do we all agree that it has changed for the better?" Then pause and wait for your audience to confirm that, in fact, the perception of Smith Street has changed.

Now move from perception back to attitude. Ask, "Okay. Now that we all understand that Smith Street is a safe place to do business, how do we feel about starting a new business on Smith Street?"

Hopefully, here your audience will suggest that they have a new attitude toward Smith Street based on their new perceptions.

Finally, your challenge is to move from a changed attitude to a changing behavior. Say, "I think we all have a new attitude about the opportunities in starting a new business on Smith Street. How many are thinking of starting one right now?"

10

The Presentation That Builds Trust

Where large sums of money are concerned, it is advisable to trust nobody.—Agatha Christie (English author, dramatist; 1890–1976)

The toughest thing about the power of trust is that it's very difficult to build and very easy to destroy.—Thomas J. Watson, Sr. (founder of IBM; 1874–1956)

Honesty is the best policy—when there is money in it.—Mark Twain (U.S. novelist, journalist; 1835–1910)

In May 1992, Texas billionaire Ross Perot had to consider a run for the U.S. presidency. His quick wit, down-to-earth charm, and sound-bite persona had become so popular that a CNN/Time poll put him ahead of all rivals, with 33 percent of Americans saying they would vote for him, 28 percent for incumbent president George H. W. Bush, leaving only 24 percent for Arkansas governor and presidential hopeful Bill Clinton. For personal reasons Perot pulled out of the race in July, but then he jumped back in on October 1, a month before election day, to find his poll numbers had skidded to a mere 7 percent. Most wrote him off as a lost cause.

Five days later he roared back to stun the political pros. Perot bought a 30-minute time slot on CBS to air a "no frills" cardboard flipchart presentation. As 16.5 million Americans watched, Perot talked directly to the camera, described the decline in the American economy, and hand flipped his own chart cards at the rate of about one a minute.

Ad Age magazine columnist Bob Garfield described the result: "Proving again that the best selling is actual selling, the 30-minute format enables Perot to do for economic reality what the "Amazing Discoveries" infomercial did for car finish. He doesn't set fire to the hood, but he does open it up and let us see the wreck underneath."

The "wreck underneath" was the American economy. Perot bluntly laid out a chilling scenario of a nation headed for steep economic decline. He kept on point as he described American high-tech manufacturing: "We don't have a plan or strategy. We'd better get one.... Y'say, 'Oh, but Ross, we'll always make the commercial airliners for the world' [leaning toward the camera]... Don't bet on it."

Perot made the risk of picking the wrong president look very dangerous, and since he was the only one talking about these problems, he seemed like the guy you could most likely trust to fix them. On Election Day, one in five Americans voted for the man with the "no-frills" flipcharts, making Perot the most successful independent presidential candidate in U.S. history.

HOW THIS WORKS

When the stakes are high in a decision, so is the risk. As your audience decides on a course of action, the greater the risk involved, the more likely they will choose the option with the outcome they trust the most.

Pitfalls

Mistaking Personal Trust for Functional Trust

As a presenter trying to persuade an audience, you are asking for change, and all change involves risk. During your presentation you will be focused on what you say and show, but your audience will be more concerned with what happens afterward. To an audience concerned with risk, trust is about what happens after your presentation is over, if they say "yes." There are many aspects to trust, but as it relates to a 20-minute presentation, trust is primarily about reassuring your audience about the outcome of what you advocate and managing the perception of risk.

As Dow, Napolito, and Pusateri wrote in *The Trust Imperative,* published by The Strategic Account Management Association: "Without risk, trust serves little purpose since not much is at stake. Risk generally stems from uncertainty about an important future outcome, or because one party is highly dependent on another party."

Thinking You Can Just Tell People to Trust You

Lew Hoff, CEO of Bartizan Corporation, once received a presentation from a financial services company that spent half an hour showing him the services they could offer. When Hoff told the presenter that he could get these same services from his current supplier, the presenter replied, "Well, there is a really big difference. That difference is me. And you're just going to have to trust me on that." Hoff stayed with his current supplier. Maybe it's human nature, maybe it's the clichés about used car salesmen, but no one trusts the presenter who says, "Trust me."

Step by Step: Preparation

Evaluate Audience Risk

Ask yourself, "If my audience accepts what I propose, what do they risk?"

Not all risk is financial. Switching to a new cell phone service with poor coverage can be inconvenient, voting for a candidate who switches allegiances can be frustrating, buying into a technology that becomes obsolete can cause technical problems. Even switching product brands of small purchases that go bad can make you look foolish in front of friends, peers, or spouses. No one likes to think they're a "sucker."

Think about the worst thing that could happen to an audience that accepts your plan. Then think about how you can reassure them that this will not happen.

Anticipate the Trust Level

How much time should you plan on trust-building activity? The answer varies greatly, depending on where the audience's trust level is at the start. I fondly remember a presentation I gave at the national sales meeting of a media company where I was a salesperson. Sales meetings are always upbeat affairs, and I was introduced as a local hero who had broken all the sales records. Since I knew almost everyone in the audience, my connection with them was instantaneous and every joke I told got a big laugh.

In contrast, I recently gave a presentation at a competitive media day. I was one of 12 magazine representatives, each given 20 minutes to present their competitive case. In a Manhattan boardroom I faced an audience of seven strangers, intentionally rotated in their jobs to prevent them from developing any relationship with salespeople. Nothing I said was taken at face value, everything I said was suspect, and the assumption was that I was selling a commodity and trying to bamboozle them into thinking I had something unique.

I planned for these two presentations differently. At my media day, most of my time was spent on trust building; at my sales meeting, not much at all.

Plan to Build "Moments of Trust"

Personal trust between people takes time to develop, often months or years. During that time, trust is built up bit by bit through a series of small incidents or "moments of trust" where two people find or share common values, interests, experiences, successes, or feelings. Trust results from the cumulative effect of these "moments of trust" over time.

In the context of a 20-minute presentation your challenge is to compress the same process as described above into the limited time you have. This can be done if you plan a series of "moments of trust" within your presentation. As in real life, their cumulative effect can create a sense of trust, at least as it relates to you and your presentation.

The goal is to create small incidents throughout your presentation where your audience comes to see and believe in you and what you are sharing. Here are some typical "moments of trust," based on human nature, that have been used in presentations.

People Trust What Is Familiar. I was selling a new technology, a sponsored Webcast, to an audience of technophobes. I said: "Don't be intimidated by the technology. Believe it or not, you already know what a Webcast is and how it works. It's just like a sponsored educational seminar, only we do it on the Internet." Then I explained the details.

If you can find a way for your audience to understand what you are proposing in the context of something with which they are already familiar and comfortable, you can earn a moment of trust.

People Trust What They Understand. Ron Johnson, vice president of sales and marketing at Adtec Digital, brought an understanding of video compression to an audience for the first time. He asked everyone in his audience to take out a sheet of paper and write some numbers on it. Then he asked everyone to wad up the paper and throw it across the room. For a few minutes it was chaos as people in the back of the room threw their paper to the front and vice versa. Finally Johnson said: "Now pick up one of those paper wads, open it up and read it. What you just did is how video compression works. You took a message, compressed it, sent it, and now, when you opened your wad of paper you have just decompressed it."

There may be aspects of your product or option about which your audience is fuzzy. If you can be the one to clarify these and help them understand, you can earn a moment of trust.

People Trust What Seems Objective. As Steve Fayer began scripting a PBS documentary on the life of Ford Motor Company founder Henry Ford at the time of the Great Depression, he found conflicting facts about Ford's life. Initially, Fayer considered Ford a controversial figure, as history recalls Ford during those years as a man violently opposed to the labor movement and who had both anti-Semitic and pro-Nazi sympathies. But Fayer was surprised to find a survey of Americans taken at the time that chose Ford as the third greatest man that had ever lived, behind only Jesus Christ and Napoleon.

Fayer scripted the story to include both sides, believing that by including what he calls "testimony against interest," or information that contrasts the presentation's prevailing point of view, it would make the presentation stronger. Explains Fayer: "If you are telling a story, particularly if you have an axe to grind, you'd better be sure that you hear from the other side of it, otherwise people won't believe you. Including 'testimony against interest' makes your story legitimate and builds audience confidence in you."

If you give competitive options a fair shake (perhaps over a less important aspect), it can earn a moment of trust.

People Trust What Feels Real. Jerry White, cofounder of the Landmine Survivors Network, has the challenge of making the threat of landmines seem real to people without turning them off with stories of blood and gore. White started one presentation by telling the audience that before he personally was a victim of a landmine attack he, like his audience, had no idea what a landmine even looked like. After explaining how a landmine works, he passed a sample landmine through the audience to make his description very tangible and his point very real.

If you can find a way to make the point you are advocating seem very real to your audience, you can earn a moment of trust.

People Trust What They Personally Experience. John Torrey, now director of NAFTA (North America Free Trade Agreement) Affairs at Yellow Transportation, took on a big challenge years ago while working at a large media company. He was assigned to get sales-people from different departments to cooperate on joint sales pro-posals. Up until then, there had been no communication between these departments, so salespeople were skeptical about joint sales proposals because they thought they did not have clients in com-mon with other departments. Torrey was given a speaking slot at a companywide sales meeting to change that perception.

Torrey began his presentation with an exercise. He asked everyone in the audience to turn around in their seat and find someone from a different department with whom to pair up. Then he asked these pairs to talk and see if they or their depart-ments had any clients in common. For the next five minutes, conversation buzzed though the auditorium. When Torrey asked for a show of hands to see how many had found accounts in common, about two-thirds of the hands went up. After that, no salesperson could ignore Torrey's program. They had all experi-enced finding mutual clients together.

If you can get your audience to experience part of what you advocate, you can earn a moment of trust.

People Trust What Can Be Proven. Said Henry David Thoreau, "No way of thinking or doing, however ancient, can be trusted without proof." If you can find ways to prove the major points of your presentation, you will earn moments of trust. (For more on using facts and proof, please refer to Chapter 7.)

People Trust What Is Guaranteed. If your product or option comes with a guarantee, be prepared to discuss it. If there is no formal guarantee, think about what you can share to assure results. You can earn a moment of trust if you can make your assurances stick.

Step by Step: Giving the Presentation

Make a Good First Impression Instantly... or Else

Before an audience can trust your presentation, they have to trust you. Be aware that your audience will evaluate your trustworthiness instantly. Rob Galford, president of Trusted Advisor Associates, says that within 30 seconds of seeing you they have already decided if they can trust you or not. Adds Galford, "After that, you have the next 19 seconds to either help people confirm it or disprove it, and it's easier to confirm than disprove."

On a subconscious level your audience's minds rush to judgment even faster. Dr. Tania Singer and Joel S. Winston of the University College London's Institute of Neurology have found that the decision to trust or not, on a subconscious level, takes milliseconds. They have used brain scans to measure human reaction to portraits of various people. They discovered that our minds make an instant judgment as to "friend or foe" milliseconds after we meet a new person, and well before our cognitive minds are engaged. They speculate that this is a defense mechanism buried in our subconscious minds that helped our prehistoric ancestors stay alive.

In other studies where subjects reviewed a variety of people photos, respondents consistently picked as "most trustworthy" photos of people who most looked like themselves. It may sound superficial, but for better or worse, we tend to trust people who look, dress, and talk like ourselves. As Thomas J. Watson, Sr., founder of IBM, said almost 100 years ago: "The essence of trust building is to emphasize the similarities between you and the customer."

Think about ways you can come to be seen as "similar" to your audience.

People Trust People Whose Dress Is Similar

As David Zaus and Donna Downes of Zaus Downes Inc. planned a presentation that would include a CEO of a Fortune 25 corporation, they invested in some extremely high-end clothing. Downes said: "Appearance can make a big difference. It's amazing. All of a sudden, you're wearing what they're wearing and they feel much more comfortable with you."

Dressing worse than your audience will create a poor first impression, and dressing a lot better can create distance. When your audience first sees you, if you are dressed like they are, they will trust you more.

People Trust People Whose Language Is Similar

Many audiences share a common language that binds them together. For example:

→ Chemical engineers share a language of technical terms.
→ Soccer enthusiasts share a language of sports terms.
→ Environmentalists share a language that implies a love of the earth.

→ A political action group can share the language of anger or passion.

If you can speak your audience's "language," they will trust you more.

Listen for Trust "Hot" Buttons

I once gave a presentation to a buying committee with whom it seemed I could do nothing right. They crossed me on every point I made, pushed me hard for concessions that were clearly unreasonable, and finally got rude and nasty. It got so bad that I actually gave up even wanting them as a client. Finally I blew up and yelled: "This is the worst treatment I have ever had from a buying committee. I have shown you the best product at the best price you are ever going to find. Go buy something else that costs 5 cents less if you like! This is as far as we go!" As I hastily began packing my presentation materials the head buyer ran up to me, put an arm around my shoulder and said: "Not so fast Josh. We really liked what you said. Sorry about pushing so hard. But we do this to everyone who comes here. How else can we trust that you are giving us the best possible deal?"

Luckily, not every audience establishes their sense of trust by pushing suppliers to the emotional break point, but every audience does have some way that they evaluate the trustworthiness of a presenter. I have presented to groups that later told me they trust presenters only if

→ *"You do not trash your competition."* As I once began to talk about a competitor, I saw frowns cross the faces of my audience. I realized I was about to cross a line beyond which my audience would trust me less. I changed direction and later found out that the CEO of the company to which I was presenting had issued an edict that any salespeople who trashed their competition while calling on his company were not to be trusted or bought from.

➜ *"You have experience in our industry."* Once, toward the end of a lengthy presentation, I was battered by many detailed questions about the industry my audience was in. I found out later that they already knew the answers to the questions; they just wanted to know if *I* did. One said, "How can we trust you will be able to follow through on your proposal unless you understand our industry?"

➜ *"You don't waste our time."* I was once given 15 minutes to make a presentation. I was alarmed when, with five minutes to go, several managers in my audience looked at their watches. With only minutes left, I asked if I was boring them and should talk about something else. One manager smiled widely and said, "No, keep going. We just want to make sure you respect our time." When my 15 minutes were up, I was told, "Before we waste an hour and a half of our team's time we need to trust that you will not waste it. You passed the test. We have another hour. What else would you like to show us?"

Often your audience does not know themselves how they evaluate trust, they just do it. But if you can figure it out, you can respond to it.

I have also presented to audiences who would trust you only if

➜ You will fight for your option with passion
➜ Your shoes are well cared for and polished

→ You are extremely well prepared
→ They like you personally
→ You carry an expensive pen (Mont Blanc preferred)

There are many ways to evaluate trust. If you listen and watch your audience closely, they will tell you what you need to know. Bette Davis, the famous Hollywood actress from the 1930s, said, "Never, never trust anyone who asks for white wine. It means they're phonies."

Watch Out for the "Entitlement Devil"

Gerhardt Schwantner, publisher of *SellingPower* magazine, says many presenters lose audience trust because they believe they are entitled to a great reception. Schwanter says: "It becomes an entitlement issue because you have invested the time, paid for a plane ticket, and prepared a PowerPoint presentation. After you have made that up-front investment, the feeling is that you are entitled to the meeting running on time, to all the members of your audience showing up, to everybody paying attention, and to everyone being interested. If you feel entitled to all of those things and they don't happen, you can get disappointed or frustrated. That can leak through in a negative, resentful, sulking attitude that kills your presentation. In my view, that kills more presentations than anything else."

Watch Your Self-Interest

Rob Galford, president of Trusted Advisor Associates, has a formula he uses to evaluate an audience's level of trust. It begins with three familiar elements—credibility, reliability, and intimacy—that, taken together, build trust. So far, so good. But Galford then advocates that the collective impact that these three will have on your audience is decreased and divided by the degree of self-interest your audience sees in you.

Galford's trust formula:

$$\frac{\text{Credibility} + \text{Reliability} + \text{Intimacy}}{\text{Your self-interest}}$$

Self-interest, when it shows up, can badly undermine all the other elements of trust that you worked so hard to establish.

When I received my first sales training, long ago, I was given bad advice: I was told to use a lot of manipulative closing techniques. Obvious sales techniques are blatant signs of self-interest. They destroy trust quickly. You may want the business badly, but if you make your presentation all about you needing their business, instead of about your audience needing what you are presenting, trust is lost.

Closing

When an audience comes to trust you, the room feels different: the skeptical looks go away, what you say is accepted at face value, and questions become more about opportunities than about "what could go wrong."

A trusting audience is calmer, more accepting, and more willing to take a risk with you. When they have reached this point, it is time to ask them to take that risk. You may not see accepting your product or option as a risk, but audiences with big trust issues will.

As in many closes to presentations, this one will be a summary—a summary of reassurances. It is time to review the reasons they should accept your product or option, and then review all of the reassurances that came out, planned or unplanned, during the presentation.

Finally, and just before you ask them for the order, it's important to frame all of your reassurances with a statement that you are in this process for the long haul. In other words, after they say "yes," that you or your organization will be there to support their decision. Your job is to make it understood that you're here for the long haul if something goes wrong.

Then simply ask them to accept what you have proposed. If they trust you and they trust what you have presented, they are likely to say, "Yes!"

11

The Presentation That
Offers a Solution

A problem well stated is a problem half solved.—Charles Kettering (U.S. engineer, inventor; 1876–1958)

It's so much easier to suggest solutions when you don't know too much about the problem.—Malcolm Forbes (U.S. publisher, editor; 1919–1990)

The most exciting phrase to hear in science, the one that heralds new discoveries, is not 'Eureka! (I found it!)' but rather, "hmm… that's funny…"—Isaac Asimov (U.S. science writer, science fiction writer; 1920–1992)

In 1980 the rapidly growing personal computer (PC) industry hit a billion dollars and IBM, the world's largest computer company, wanted in. But IBM had a problem. They were arriving late and had to get in fast before the PC industry grew too large without them.

A task force within IBM broke with many traditions by winning the go-ahead to rush a PC to market using outside suppliers. In August, Jack Sams, a task force member, phoned the president of the small company that led the PC industry in computer languages and asked for an appointment. "How about next week?" the company president offered. Said Sams, "We'd like to be there tomorrow."

Sams arrived with his group and recalled that "a young fella" came to take them back to the president's office." At first Sams thought he was the office boy, an easy mistake to make since Microsoft's president, Bill Gates, was only 24 years old at the time.

Sams tested Gates's resolve immediately by putting a nondisclosure agreement on the table. IBM was moving quickly but wanted to keep their entry into the PC market a secret. Gates signed immediately. Then, without revealing the nature of their project, Sams started asking questions. Gates shared openly, demonstrating his tremendous knowledge and insight, even describing what he thought a great personal computer would look like. Sams was dazzled by his presentation and returned to IBM calling Gates one of the most brilliant men he had ever met, and highly recommended using his company.

A month later, Sams and his group returned to Microsoft ready to buy. After agreeing that IBM would license an array of Microsoft computer languages, Sams asked if they could also supply the computer's operating system. But Microsoft did not make operating systems. Gates, nervous that his huge computer language order would disappear if IBM didn't find a suitable operating system quickly set up a a next-day visit with Gary Kindall, CEO of Digital Research, the leading maker of PC operating systems.

But when Sams and his group arrived at Digital Research, Kindall was out on business. Kindall's wife was in charge, and she became rattled when Sams pulled out his nondisclosure agreement. She refused to sign it until a lawyer reviewed it. A lawyer arrived hours later and the meeting focused on the nondisclosure agreement, not on solving IBM's problems. Eventually Sams and his team left without ever talking to Kindall.

Back at Microsoft, Bill Gates saw the opportunity of a lifetime. Being on the inside of IBM's problem, he knew what IBM needed in an operating system and understood their timetable and secrecy issues. In addition, he had been presold to IBM's top management. Instead of bickering over legalities, Gates successfully offered Sams a problem-solving package that included computer language licenses and an operating system all delivered on a tight deadline. Short on time, Microsoft bought an operating system from another small software company and reworked it, naming it MS-DOS, the operating system that would run the IBM PC.

The IBM PC went on to become a huge success, and Microsoft's operating system rode it to become the most popular in the PC business. Digital Research's CP/M operating system was pushed out of the market and eventually disappeared. Bill Gates went on to build a business worth billions whose core product was, and still is, computer operating systems.

HOW THIS WORKS

Problem solvers are not chosen solely for their ability to find solutions. A large part of winning a solution-based presentation is demonstrating a working relationship with

your audience during the presentation process itself. Every audience that chooses a solution is also choosing a relationship with a solution provider.

In 1980, almost every personal computer not made by Apple ran on Gary Kindall's operating system, CPM. If IBM chose their solution provider on experience alone, Microsoft never would have been picked.

The best way to become the problem solver of choice is to get inside your audience's problem and develop a plan that nails the problem cold. Then you can say, "Okay this is the plan, we came up with it using your input and it's everything you need. If you hire us to implement this it will get done right, or you can take a chance with someone else."

Pitfalls

Assuming Your Audience Knows What Their Problems Are

Selling a solution is often about diagnosing a problem for which you can then provide an answer. Many times you can do this by being an outside source of expertise that raises awareness to an opportunity. As Albert Einstein said, "Problems cannot be solved at the same level of awareness that created them."

Not Realizing That Most of the Obvious Problems Have Been Solved

Most of the solutions I have sold are for problems my audience did not know they had. If you wait around for organizations to realize they have a problem and call you, you will be waiting a long time. There is far more opportunity to solve latent or future problems than ones that have already been clearly identified.

Step by Step: Preparation

Prepare to "Work Your Way In"

For individuals, talking about problems can be embarrassing. For organizations, admitting to problems that become public can mean trouble, if competitors talk about them to mutual customers. Michel Proulx, vice president of product development at Miranda Technologies, says, "You can't call someone up and say, 'What's your problem?' That never works. In fact, it turns people off."

While there is a natural resistance to sharing information about problems, if you can convince your audience that you can really help them with their problems and can be trusted to keep confidences, the floodgates will open. There is a basic need and desire to talk about problems with someone who can really help. "The place to connect with someone is at their problem space. They will easily forget what your product is, but they'll never forget what their problem is," says Proulx.

First, Define the Context

Problem solving begins with your audience's context, or your audience's situation as it relates to your area of expertise. Michel Proulx describes context in many ways: "Context is what your customers do on a day-to-day basis in the area you want to problem solve in. It could be the area they are having trouble with. It could be the thing they are trying to achieve. It could be an application they are looking for."

Get Them to Talk about Their Context or Situation

Before you present, you have to get people who represent your audience to talk to you about their situation. The more they talk, the more you'll know, and the more targeted your initial presentation will be. If you have an established relationship and a proven track record, getting people to share will be easy. If not, do your homework and prepare to sell yourself in this first step. Proulx recommends starting with a casual conversation where you ask questions. He says, "A great way to get them to talk about their problems is to describe similar problems you have helped solve in the past."

If you cannot even have a phone conversation about this, try one of the following strategies that I have used:

→ A back-and-forth e-mail exchange, where you ask questions
→ A short visit at a trade show booth
→ Using a secretary as intermediary, where questions are shuttled between you and the boss

Look for a "Problem" to Solve

During your conversation about your audience's situation, you should be looking for a problem to solve. But don't limit yourself to just overt problems. As you hear about your audience's situation, listen for opportunities to problem-solve in any area you can play a part in. Besides overt problems, consider

→ A way to accelerate growth
→ A way to transition to a new technology or system
→ Improvement in possibilities
→ A way to improve efficiency
→ A way to bring in more customers or new business

→ A way to help with cash flow
→ A way to become more competitive
→ A way to prevent a future problem your audience has not considered
→ A way to save money immediately or over time

If you are just looking for "problems" in the narrow sense of the word, you will limit the solutions you can offer.

Make Assumptions

Once you know about your audience's situation you can start to combine it with knowledge of your capabilities and look for matches. Here is where you have to make assumptions. For example, while selling ad space, if I discover a company that has picked up a new, aggressive competitor I will make the assumption that they want to increase ad expenditures to fend off the new threat.

Try filling in these blanks to start thinking about assumptions you can make:

If they are going to _____,
they will need _____.

When _____ comes,
they will need _____.

To stay competitive when _____ happens,
they will need _____.

Assumptions can be powerful tools in the problem-solving process. When IBM first contacted Bill Gates, they did not share their secret plan to build a personal computer. But Gates made the assumption that IBM would not be calling a company with Microsoft's capabilities unless they were seriously looking to be a player in the personal computer market. With that assumption in mind, Gates conducted himself accordingly in his first meeting with IBM with great success; Gary Kindall did not.

Prepare an Initial Presentation

It is always easier to react to a proposed solution than to construct one from scratch. An initial presentation provides a sounding board by offering a solution as a work in progress. Solutions always require customization, and the best way to flesh out the details is to present one and see how your audience reacts. After your initial, exploratory conversations about your audience's situation, three scenarios, described below, can emerge.

1. A Single Solution Seems Obvious. If one obvious solution emerges, present it. Douglas B. Leeds, president of the Tori Group, has a great approach to doing this. Leeds enthusiastically takes his audience step by step through the same process of discovery that led him to the solution he is presenting. Says Leeds: "Sharing my thought process gives them ownership in what I've concluded. It is so much more powerful than just making a recommendation." He concludes, "If my idea is the right one, it should be the logical, correct answer." There is a side benefit to this approach: While sharing it in the first person you build personal credibility. Says Leeds: "If I am successful, I have also presented myself as being professional and thoughtful. This puts me in a more authoritative position."

2. Several Solutions Have Merit. A few years back, Michael Clinton, executive vice president and publishing director at

Hearst Magazines, was challenged by the Milk Processors Association (who produced the "Got Milk" campaign), for a solution to a competitive situation. At the time, there were many new kinds of waters and sodas that were entering the beverage market. The milk processors wanted to keep milk top of mind and keep consumption high.

Clinton's group was one of 25 media organizations invited to present solutions. First came an informal meeting with the association's media group. Clinton recalls: "During a dialogue across the table we asked questions. We asked, 'What does your client need? What is the problem that needs to be solved? What is the solution that needs to be realized?'"

Using this feedback, Clinton's group worked up three approaches to be presented at their next meeting. Clinton said, "We presented the three concepts right away and got a reaction on each of them. When they said, 'We like this one the best,' we put the other two on the side and went deeper into the one they picked."

Then Clinton's team spent a good hour discussing in detail how the idea could be implemented, element by element. The final presentation contained an explanation of the program along with implementation and cost details. It was done on PowerPoint and left behind for review. Not only did Clinton's group win the competition but their program went on to help differentiate milk as a beverage and sell over 200,000 extra gallons of milk.

Presenting several solutions is a great way to go when there are several approaches that might work. Not only do you avoid putting all your eggs in one basket, but it also helps get your audience involved as they react to different elements in each one.

3. *Not Enough Feedback to Pick a Solution.* If you cannot get enough direction from anyone as to what solution you should prepare to present, do not be discouraged. Often these situations present the biggest opportunities. But your preparation needs to shift. You need to turn part of your presentation time into a probing session. Here are some approaches to consider:

FOCUS ON THEIR SITUATION OR CONTEXT. I start by saying, "I am familiar with your organization and your situation. Does what I am about to tell you sound right?" Then, because I have prepared well, I describe my audience's situation in detail while scrupulously avoiding saying anything about my products or solutions. Talking about their situation is serious bait for getting feedback. Here you are, an out-of-towner, describing their neighborhood. If you just focus on their particulars, they will start to pipe up. They will agree with some of your observations and disagree with others.

Once I have them talking about their situation, I work in some questions. People like to talk about themselves and their situation, and by asking questions I give them the chance to do so. I ask:

→ How do you think your situation will change?
→ How *has* it changed?
→ What problems do you have now?
→ What problems do you anticipate?
→ Who are your competitors?
→ How is business?

I do all this without bringing up my product or any solution. If my audience asks for a product detail, I respond quickly but then steer the discussion right back to their situation. Other salespeople I have worked with hate this. They want to jump in and give their product pitch at the first sign of opportunity to close business. I find that the moment when salespeople are typically trained to start closing is often the same moment when the consultative part of the dialogue begins to emerge.

By returning to focus on my audience's situation I always get a bigger picture of their business. Selling solutions is not about catching a fish quickly so you can move on to catch the next fish. Solution selling is about understanding the bigger picture so you can fit your product or option into a larger solution. Keeping the dialogue on your customer's situation longer will help you catch a much, much bigger fish.

Then, you will start to see opportunities to apply your capabilities. If you come up with a solution in real time that solves a problem for the first time, there is great magic and theater in it. Your audience will find instant ownership of a solution that emerges from these conversations.

SHARE A NUMBER OF SOLUTIONS IN SUMMARY FORM. After I've been presenting solutions in an industry for several years I generally have a laptop full of presentations that describe different solutions my audiences have used. I use these presentations as bait for new customers in the following way: I will pick the five solutions I anticipate a particular audience might like best. Then I tell that audience that I have five different presentations of solutions on my laptop and that I am going to give them a four-minute summary of each, then show them the presentation of the solution in which they are most interested. I have used this approach dozens of times and have never actually showed any of these audiences the presentations on my laptop. Every time, the audience likes a part of one solution and mixes it with parts of others to create a custom solution that is unique to their company's needs.

Step by Step: The Initial Presentation

The Deeper You Get In, the Deeper You Get In

The goal of the initial presentation is to probe for more information, demonstrate your capabilities, show that you did your homework, and motivate your audience to help shape a solution that becomes your final proposal.

In your initial presentation, your performance is as important as your presentation. While your audience does not expect you to get right away every detail about their situation, you must establish right away a rapport with them. Problem solving is not a tangible product, and the problem-solving relationship you offer is as important as the solution itself.

The initial presentation gives the audience a chance to "try on" that relationship. They will see how you think, and how you react to their feedback. They will see, in real time, if you bring (or don't bring) ideas, perspective, analysis, or insight to the table that has value. If you can't say anything that is totally on target, say something interesting, original, or something your audience has not heard before you will miss this opportunity.

Showtime

Since solutions only have meaning when put into a context, Miranda Technologies' Michel Proulx suggests starting by describing the context and getting your audience to agree with your description. Proulx says, "In my presentations, 50 percent will be about context, 40 percent will be product detail, and 10 percent will be competitive positioning."

Proulx is a legendary PowerPoint wizard who uses the medium to its fullest. For explaining context and applications he suggests using a "build sequence." This is a series of slides in which the first has very little on it, and each successive slide has the same content but with a bit more added to it. One slide could contain the situation without the proposed solution, and the next few slides could show that same view but with each one adding a bit more detail until we see the whole solution.

For Proulx, the best solution presentation unfolds as if he were a mind reader. "If we had the right intelligence before and we interpreted it correctly, we can often create a presentation that anticipates an audience's reaction. When they ask a question, I advance to the next slide, where the answer is explained. It's not ESP; it comes from forcing yourself to put the context and application first, so by the time you describe your solution it becomes a logical progression."

What If You Misread Context?

Proulx advises that when you misread context, go to the whiteboard and ask your audience to describe exactly what their situation is. Admit temporary defeat and ask for help. Later, if you have a library of presentations on your laptop, you can regroup, pick the one most appropriate, and get on with the show.

Closing

With large, complex proposals like the one on which Michael Clinton's group worked, the close requires the development of a second presentation based on feedback from the first. The goal is to modify the original solution so that when you present it, very few changes will be necessary for your audience to accept it on the spot.

With smaller solutions, adapting the original proposal on the spot will often gain commitment from the audience. Either way, when you have your audience's feedback incorporated into your proposal, explain the new proposal to your audience. Then focus their attention on a summary of that modified proposal either by reading it aloud or by walking them through a prepared slide on the screen. After that, say, "We have worked hard together to come up with this solution and it addresses your specific needs. Can we move forward with this?" If you have done your homework, come up with relevant ideas, and captured insightful feedback from your audience, the answer will be "yes."

12

The Presentation That Makes a Financial Case

Money is a singular thing. It ranks with love as man's greatest source of joy. And with death as his greatest source of anxiety. Over all history it has oppressed nearly all people in one of two ways: either it has been abundant and very unreliable, or reliable and very scarce.—John Kenneth Galbraith (author, economist; 1908–)

All money is a matter of belief.—Adam Smith (economist; 1723–1790)

A fool and her money are soon courted.—Helen Rowland (American writer; 1875–1950)

In 1957 Akio Morita, cofounder of the tiny Japanese electronic firm Tokyo Tsushin Kogyo, came to New York to sell his company's products. When a large retail chain asked for pricing of his transistor radios at volume levels up to 100,000 units, Morita faced a problem. His factory could only handle an order for 10,000 units. Taking a much larger order would mean hiring new employees and building new facilities, both of which would likely be idle after the order was filled. In Japan at the time, laying off workers was considered unacceptable, so taking the order could easily overextend Morita's small company.

Morita also feared that taking too big an order would make it hard to fill orders for other customers. In his hotel room that night he struggled with his presentation and laid out a financial proposal that motivated the buyer to serve his longer-term vision. When the buyer saw Morita's numbers, he was flabbergasted.

Morita offered 5,000 radios at the regular price, and a discount for 10,000 units. But at 30,000 units the price went up; at 50,000 pieces his price was higher than the 5,000-unit price, and at 100,000 units the price was higher still!

At first the buyer did not know what to think. He had never even heard of Morita's company and could barely pronounce its name. He told Morita his proposal was illogical. Then Morita explained his own logic. The buyer smiled and placed an order for 10,000 transistor radios, exactly what Morita had hoped for.

Next year, in January 1958, with that same eye to the future, Tokyo Tsushin Kogyo changed its name to one Morita's retail buyer could pronounce and remember: Sony Corporation.

HOW THIS WORKS

Many audiences make their decisions from the bottom line up. The best way to win them over is to present your product or option so its financial benefit motivates them to accept your proposal.

Pitfalls

Thinking That Just Because the Numbers Work, You Don't Have to Sell Them on Your Story or Idea

You may take pride in the fact that your proposal delivers a full 10 percent return on investment (ROI) or profit margin, but you may be competing with three other proposals that will deliver the same return. The great strength to the financial presentation is that it forces you to be objective and present your benefits as objective financial results. This can also be a great weakness. If you are delivering 10 percent and so are four competitors, your product or option can become a commodity.

Meeting the economic criteria is only part of the process of making a financial presentation. Selling is still selling.

Thinking There Is No Emotion at the "Bottom Line"

Money is not always about profit. Money is an emotionally charged subject that can mean very different things to different organizations and people.

I have presented to all of the following:

➡ A politically charged government agency where money was a way of keeping score of internal political power. Profit was not an issue at this government agency, but money had tremendous importance as the way to build more political power within the organization. A bigger budget meant more people reporting to you and more political power. The department with the biggest budget wins!

➡ A struggling association in a down market where money was viewed like water to a man dying of thirst in the desert. Money was their very means of survival, parceled out tiny bits at a time. Here, money meant a means to survive.

➡ An organization riding the winds of change in a rapidly growing high-tech sector. As the cash piled up, money became the scorecard by which they justified their vision and their boldness, reaffirming their destiny as leaders. Here money meant a reaffirmation of success.

Consider the emotional implications of money to your audience. Ask, "emotionally, what does money mean to this audience?"

Step by Step: Preparation

First, Understand Your Audience's Business Model and Financial Goals

I once proposed that a major manufacturer run advertising to support a new product. I assumed that more sales would mean more profit. Early in my presentation I was interrupted and told there was no profit associated with this product. It was introduced as a loss leader to attract interest for other products that were profitable. Their goal was to attract as much publicity as possible while selling as few units as possible. My presentation was asking my audience to spend more money to lose more money!

If you are dealing with a publicly held company, you can view an annual report, often online, to get a better understanding of its financial goals. If there is no public financial data, a few questions asked by phone before you arrive can save you the embarrassment I felt that day.

Ask:

→ *"When does your fiscal year start?"* Money and budgets run in cycles. If you are ultimately going to ask for money, it helps to know when it can become available.

→ *"What are your economic goals and how do you plan to achieve them?"*

→ *"When will you make the economic decision?"*

→ *"How do you make your profit?"* This is not always obvious.

→ *"Which sections of your business are most profitable?"* This is a key question to help you see where the organization's internal priorities might be. If you can align your proposal to the internal priorities of the organization, you will be more successful.

→ *"Are revenues up or down from last year?"* The economic climate of the company will affect the reception your proposal receives.

→ *"Do you forecast them up or down for next year?"* If things are looking up in the future, keep this in mind if your proposal is shot down today.

→ *"How is your company stock doing?"* Good or bad news will trickle down to your proposal somehow.

→ *"How are you doing against your competition?"* Since many organizations watch their competitors more closely than they do their customers, this could have a huge impact.

When you understand how your audience intends to meet its financial goals and lay out priorities, you can build an ROI presentation that has sticking power. More ROI presentations fail because they are not aligned with the audience's business model or goals.

Find "The Number"

When Dennis Triola, group publisher at Primedia Business, proposes the launch of a new product within his group, he first gets his numbers lined up. For his department, he is aware of "the number," the profit margin target his management expects his products to achieve. Triola knows that if his presentation can show how to get to the number, he typically gets speedy approval.

Triola starts with the number and works backward from it. He lines up anticipated expenses against income and, with simple arithmetic, arrives at his projected profit margin. If the numbers don't add up, he adjusts them until they do.

Christian Tremblay, CEO of the high-tech startup Algolith, gives presentations to attract venture capital. In his world, the number, or expected returns, can be high. Says Tremblay, "When these people place money in your company, it's not because they like you. It's because they want to get money back. They want to place money in your company at the early stage, in hopes that within five years your company will be worth $100 million."

Sometimes the number is arrived at through a dialogue that you initiate. Before Jim Beckley, vice president of Channel Sales at Intrado Corporation, goes in to sell his digital security services, he analyzes the target company to see if his products can offer a strong financial benefit. By analyzing a company's size, competitive position, regulatory pressures, and corporate issues, Beckley can often predict how strong an ROI case he will be able to offer. When he contacts the company, he asks questions to find out what kind of payback will get them excited and how soon they expect it.

With a financial presentation, whenever possible, start your planning by finding the number on which you intend to close.

Translate Your Benefits into Financial Terms

When Jim Dickson, vice president of national accounts for the cable TV Inspiration Networks, visits with cable system operators who have a religious orientation, he creates interest and excitement about adding his network to their cable system by talking up his programming. Many of the commentators on Dickson's networks are well known in religious circles, as are many of the shows themselves.

But when there is no affinity for the content, Dickson changes gears and makes his presentation about delivering a financial benefit. Cable systems make most of their money from charging cable subscribers, so the more subscribers, the better. Dickson demonstrates ROI by giving examples of cable systems that have added his network and picked up new subscribers. He also shares success stories about new subscription campaigns based on the addition of his network that have added new subscribers not served by other programming. Says Dickson, "It all becomes a very bottom-line decision." Dickson's bottom-line approach has even persuaded the cable system in Las Vegas (yes, "Sin City") to carry the Inspiration Networks.

To bring forward the financial benefit, focus on the economic impact your product or option will have, if it is accepted. But what if your product or option does not translate easily? Many products or options do not have an obvious ROI story, and you'll have to work harder to find one. The following are two approaches.

Measure Something Nonfinancial but Valuable. While selling trade magazine ad space during a media recession in 2002, I was told point blank by several media buying committees to come up with an ROI story or be cut from their media schedules. It is hard to nail down the financial ROI of trade advertising. A company's sales are typically the result of a communication mix that includes trade advertising along with a Web site presence, online ads, direct mail, telemarketing, and even their sales staff. Separating out one part from that mix is very difficult.

But what can be measured is the familiarity the readers of a trade magazine develop from an advertising campaign. I offered to do a survey before and after a trade advertising campaign measuring the change in awareness of their ad message. Being able to measure how well their ad message impacted the readers of my magazine was a great piece of information to offer. While this was not a financial benefit, it was a measurable result that had value. The "R" in ROI stands for "return," and that return does not always have to be strictly financial. It does, however, have to be measurable and valuable.

What impact does your product or option have if accepted? Can you show a measurable result and then ask, "How much do you think this impact is worth?"

Pay to Measure ROI after the Fact. Often there is great evidence of your product's or option's ROI just lying around after a successful acceptance. You just have to pick it up. I once ran a series of monthly sales training sessions for the advertising sales staff of *Crain's New York Business.* While the training sessions were well received, at first, none of us realized just how successful they really were. Then, at the last session I gave the staff a survey that asked them to list specific sales made as result of the training. When the list came back we were all amazed. Hard sales directly attributed to the training were over 15 times the fee I charged. That's great ROI! My friends at Crain's were delighted and gave me a terrific testimonial that helped me sell more sales training sessions. But here's the thing: If I did not take the initiative and measure the ROI, no one would have ever known about it. The next time your product or option is successfully implemented, *pay for* a follow-up survey to measure the ROI. Then, use that information in your next presentation to make a more persuasive case.

Find Your Financial Hook

With financial presentations, there are two basic hooks, the same two that drive Wall Street and every stock exchange in the world: Fear and Greed. Here they are in action:

Fear. In 1979, Lee Iacocca became CEO of Chrysler Corporation, the third-largest automaker in the United States and a company facing certain bankruptcy. The financial situation was so shaky that Iacocca could not get banks to lend money for the turnaround he envisioned.

In an unprecedented move, Iacocca approached the U.S. Congress to guarantee $1.2 billion in loan guarantees. While

Iacocca made headlines as he testified before Congress, behind the scenes a series of financial presentations was prepared for individual congressmen. The Chrysler computers cranked out data on their suppliers of parts, services, and materials who would be hurt if Chrysler went out of business. This data was customized, congressional district by district. After the information was distributed, every congressman who would be voting on the loan guarantees knew how much money and how many jobs would be lost should the loan guarantee bill and Chrysler fail.

The motivational fear was, "If the loan guarantee bill and Chrysler fail, your district will lose money and jobs, and unemployed workers still vote." Iacocca won his loan guarantees, which, incidentally, were never needed. After he turned around Chrysler, Iacocca paid back all debts ahead of schedule.

Greed. In 1998, an unknown Merrill Lynch analyst named Henry Blodget made a ridiculous-sounding prediction: Amazon.com, then selling for $243 per share, would hit $400 per share within a year. Blodget's call got so much media attention that Amazon's stock price shot past $400 less than three weeks later. With the media following Blodget's every call, and the greed of investors following the media, the "dot-com bubble" rapidly grew. In March 2000, the Nasdaq Composite Index listing of all stocks in the tech-heavy Nasdaq stock exchange peaked at 5046.86. But the media frenzy and greed could not outrun the realities of economics. By October 2002, the Nasdaq Index had fallen 78 percent, to a low of 1114.11.

The motivational greed was "there is a new economy and the old rules of economics no longer apply. Investing in high tech is a sure way to make huge profits risk-free." Many who believed Blodget's predictions got swept up in the euphoria and subsequently burned. Blodget himself personally invested $700,000 in tech stocks days before the dot-com bubble burst, and he lost it all within a year.

Build Your Financial Story

After you bait your financial hook and describe the fiscal benefit, you need to describe how you can deliver the results. The content of your story will depend on your case.

David Rosenberg, director of Strategic Accounts and Distribution at MacDermidPrinting Solutions, starts by talking about impact; says Rosenberg, "I talk about the financial impact in numerous ways. I'll talk about it in terms of ROI, in terms of cash flow, or in terms of balance sheet impact."

While presenting to venture capital investors, Algolith CEO Christian Tremblay offers, "The presentation is like a short form of your business plan. And the business plan is just a written explanation of your presentation." While there are many ways to explain your ROI story, here are some elements that will help. You get big points if

→ You can connect your ROI message with their internal financial goals.

→ You can point to a recent example of an implementation similar to the one you are proposing that shows specific ROI results.

→ You can cite specific instances in their recent history that demonstrate your knowledge of their particular situation. Say, "Recently you have acquired ABC Corporation. How has that affected your cash flow?" The more you can position yourself as being intimately acquainted with their internal financials, the more credible you will be in presenting an economic benefit to enhance them.

→ You can find a way to offer a guarantee or assurance that the ROI you project will be met. You can either offer some kind of assurance that financial goals will be met or explain a "plan B" that shows that you are well prepared even if things go wrong.

→ You can offer some kind of measurement as part of your proposal.

→ You can give guidelines that make it easy to predict how much ROI can be expected.

→ You can clearly demonstrate your track record at delivering ROI results. For an audience evaluating the ROI you propose, the best assurance of your delivery of future results is your track record in delivering past results.

As you explain how you deliver financial results, you need to provide information that makes the process seem very real. Says David Rosenberg: "Having worked for large companies, I know how demanding they are of their people's time. At the end of the day, they're going to need a financial analysis or a business case to take to the finance department to break the dollars free. People who bring them tangible, credible information are those who they will pay attention to and whose advice they will act upon."

Toward the end of your story you will need to make financial predictions. As you make your forecasts, it is best to present only numbers you are sure to deliver, advises Strath Goodship, CEO of Miranda Technologies: "In many financial situations predictability means everything, especially if you are presenting to an audience where there has been financial instability or stress." Goodship advises understating the financial predictions to a level where results are assured. He does not see this as pessimism but rather taking a longer view. Says Goodship: "The next time you present to that audience after meeting predictions from your last meeting, you get a little bit of credibility. If you keep meeting the numbers you predict, over time, more and more of what you say will be taken at face value."

Step by Step: Giving the Presentation

Make the Numbers "Come Alive"

A great financial presentation is not a pile of static numbers, it is a dynamic living thing. The key to bring numbers to life is to present them in an interactive way. If you have prepared well, you should be able to respond to spontaneous "what-if" scenarios and demonstrate, in real time, how the numbers can be realigned to different scenarios. This often happens naturally in question-and-answer sessions.

I often present marketing budgets where someone in the audience will say, "But we are not looking for longer term brand building, we need sales results now." I say, "OK, let's adjust the budget I am proposing…." Then I move dollars out of brand building media and into more direct response media. If members of your audience do not ask questions, you may want to prepare several what-if scenarios on your own to demonstrate the dynamic nature of your numbers story.

Make the Numbers Exciting

Money is a very emotional subject. Often the emotion comes from its ability to measure or keep score in areas that are emotionally charged. Donald Trump said, "Money was never a big motivation for me, except as a way to keep score. The real excitement is playing the game."

Among the emotionally charged areas where money can "keep score" are power, prestige, attention-getting, respect, ability to help, and importance. Watch carefully for emotions in your audience as you edge closer to the point where you ask them to part with some of it. Ask yourself, "What does this money mean to this audience?"

People involved in venture capital often like the thrill of working with new ideas and dynamic people. For an audience like this, descriptions of dynamic leaders and breakthrough technologies can bring excitement.

People involved with banking often like the stability of working within a large organization. Making what you are presenting seem stable but with great potential can create the excitement of being a "great find."

I once presented to a buying committee who loved the sense of importance they had while reviewing presentations by suppliers. Showing them tremendous respect and courtesy gave them the sense of power they loved and added excitement for them.

If you can align your presentation to the emotional feelings of what money means to your audience, you can create excitement.

Respect the Emotional Life
of the Economic Decision Maker

Often the people who sign off on the economic part of the decision get little recognition. Consider Roy Disney, Walt Disney's older brother. Roy was the financial genius who helped build the Walt Disney Company. He was an equal partner with Walt from the very beginning and gave the financial guidance that led to much of that organization's success. Yet how many people know the story of Roy Disney or have even heard his name?

The economic decision makers—the accountants, vice presidents of finance, or "bean counters" —rarely get the credit they deserve. Yet, they are the ones who most often say "no" when new proposals are considered. Their perspective is that whatever new idea, project, or product comes along has to fit into the economic structure of their current organization. Whatever new option you are advocating, understand that at some time, an economic decision maker will pass judgment on your project. Show these people tremendous respect and your proposal will win approval more quickly.

I once saw a salesperson toss a page of numbers at a buying committee and quip, "here's some numbers for your bean counters." Don't do this. Take the numbers seriously and take the financial people seriously. Show them both respect in how you present and they will be allies, not obstacles.

Make Yourself and Your Organization Seem Consistent

At some point your audience is going to think, "OK, they have shown good financial results in the past and they project good results for the future, but can they deliver consistently so those projections are assured?" Financial people would love it if the ROI you project could be measured before they accept your proposal. But since no one can measure the future, consistency becomes important. Consistency bridges the gap between what can be measured in the past and what can only be predicted in the future.

As you present, your style must project consistency. If you seem disorganized, or seem to change your mind often, or jump from topic to topic, you will convey a feeling that you personally are not consistent. If you seem inconsistent, then why should they believe what you are proposing won't be?

Offer reasons as to why you deliver results in a consistent way. Talk about how you have systems that help you do this, the best analysts who have been consistently on target, policies that demand consistency, a corporate culture or a philosophy that assures consistency, or some kind of guarantee.

Closing

Put a Summary on the Screen

The last slide of a financial presentation is often a summary slide that gives a financial overview of your proposal. Leave that slide on the screen as you ask for questions.

Look for the Change in Tone

Closing an ROI presentation has to do with the numbers, but it also has to do with belief. After you have given your presentation, the cumulative effect of all the information should build confidence with your audience. When your audience starts to believe in your proposal, the tone of the room changes. Questions are focused on the upside potential, not the downside risk. Questions shift away from features and benefits and toward implementation. Members of the audience may break off into side conversations about the specifics of implementation.

Ask about the Money Timeline

Once you have an audience excited about what you propose, closing is often about timing things so the money can actually be available at the right time.

First ask, "Is this something you would like to take advantage of?"

Assuming a positive reaction, follow by asking, "How can we work out the timing so this will happen?" If you are asking for a large expenditure, it may have to be worked into the organization's budget when it comes up for annual review. You may need to follow up as next year's fiscal is being laid out. If you are asking for an audience of individuals to buy into a retirement fund, you may find they would be willing to do so around tax time but not before.

Help Them Find the Money

Sometimes closing is about finding the money within their budget. I have had intense discussions during which my audience openly admitted they did not have the money budgeted for what I proposed. We talked about other budget categories and departments that could be tapped, and other ways to structure the deal so money could come from next year's fiscal or other sources entirely.

If you can help them find the money, they will help you find the purchase order.

13

The Presentation That Gets Them to Choose You over Your Competition

Of all human powers operating on the affairs of mankind, none is greater than that of competition.—Henry Clay (U.S. politician, lawyer; 1777–1852)

A trial, like a battle, is a zero-sum game. What advantages one side disadvantages the other—and vice versa. Something that advantages both sides, but one more than the other, is a dagger directed at the side advantaged less.—David Boies (lawyer, from his book, Courting Justice; 1941–)

Competition brings out the best in products and the worst in people.—David Sarnoff (U.S. radio and television pioneer, CEO of RCA; 1891–1971)

In January 2005, Steven Jobs, CEO of Apple Corporation, took to the stage at a technology trade show to introduce a new product designed to extend Apple's popular iPod product line.

He began by telling his audience the story of how the product was created. A pie chart on the screen behind Jobs showed the digital music player market in January 2004. Apple's iPod players had 31 percent of the market. Jobs explained that at that time, Apple had introduced the iPod mini, a lower-cost unit designed to expand their sales and market share. Said Jobs, "Well, it's a year later. How'd we do? It's January 2005 and I am pleased to report that the iPod market share has doubled to 65 percent, while the flash market share has been cut in half to 29 percent..."

On the screen, pie charts contrasted 2004 and 2005 sales to emphasize the accomplishment, as a collective gasp ran though the audience. Another screen isolated just the 2005 share and contrasted the parts of the market iPod now commanded against the parts they did not. Jobs paused and asked, "So, what's next?" Indicating the remaining 29 percent of the flash player marketplace not owned by Apple, Jobs said simply, "We'd like to go after the remaining mainstream flash market." The audience, clearly on Jobs's side, crackled with laughter and spontaneous applause.

Jobs continued, "So we've taken a look at this market and it's a zoo. There's a zillion little flash players and the market's incredibly fragmented...." Another screen showed photos of five actual, but unnamed, flash players placed horizontally across the screen. Jobs described these and other current players in the market as having similar characteristics, including what he referred to as a "tortured user interface." Jobs and his design team wanted to come up with a completely new idea to make a product that was way better.

Said Jobs, "And then we saw it—it was clear as a bell." Feedback from thousands of iPod users revealed a new listening trend. Once users had loaded their favorite songs onto their iPods, the preferred way to listen to them was with the "shuffle" feature that plays songs in a random sequence. Concluded Jobs, "We decided to base a flash-based player around the shuffle. And so, today we are introducing the iPod Shuffle and this is what it looks like…"

Jobs showed the new product, emphasizing its unique small size and ease of use. Then he was back to comparisons to show the audience that this was not just a cool idea but a practical product that could win in the marketplace.

Regarding storage capability: A slide showed the five name-less flash players with their memory capacity printed above. They all had 256 megabytes of storage. The next slide showed the iPod Shuffle, with about twice that memory. Toward the end of the presentation, the unnamed flash units were shown with their memory printed above and their prices shown below. Of the five, three cost $149. One cost a little more and one a little less. When another slide showed the iPod Shuffle price of $99, the audience broke into applause.

Through hard work and innovation, Jobs showed a superior vision for his product, but it was through comparison that he demonstrated that the product had the ability to win in the current marketplace.

HOW THIS WORKS

The human mind develops a sense of value through comparison. When your audience compares your offering to that of your competition, it is important to be seen as the top pick, since no audience buys the product with the second-best overall value, votes for the candidate they like second best, or embraces the second-best solution to their problem. Influencing this process of comparison makes the difference between winning and losing.

Pitfalls

Thinking Your Audience Is a "Clean Slate"

Your audience has been formulating their perceptions of how your offering stacks up against competition long before you gave your first presentation.

Audience members may have seen a presentation from a competitor, bought or used a competitor's product, seen a trade ad campaign from another, heard a news item about one more, or had a peer recommend looking into another.

The perceptions formulated prior to your arrival may be completely inaccurate, planted by competitors, and very persistent. Most often they are easily dealt with once you arrive but can become your undoing if you ignore them.

Overtly Attacking a Competitor to Get Your Audience's Business

If you are sitting in a roomful of people who are giving business to a competitor, by attacking that competitor you may also be attacking the judgment of those people. Unless you have some direct control over your audience, criticizing the very people you want to persuade never works.

You will trigger a defensive reaction that will motivate your audience to knuckle down and justify their initial decision to buy from your competition. Long after you leave the room they will be thinking of their reasons for buying from that competitor, why they were right to do so, and what it was about your presentation that was wrong. This is not the behavior you want to encourage!

Thinking Your Audience Does Not Want You to Talk about Your Competition

Competitors may make your job harder, but your audience loves the fact that you have them. Competition keeps prices low, quality high, and innovation in constant demand. Let me repeat, your audience loves the fact that you have competition. Audiences have no toleration for presenters who complain that they have competition, attack competitors for spite or bravado, or are so focused on their competition they forget to address their audience's needs.

But audiences do not dislike all forms of competitive presenting. They need to understand your competition's weaknesses in order to make the best possible decisions. How will they find this out if you do not help them? There are ways to share this information without causing offense.

Step by Step: Preparation

Find Out Where You Stand on Their Mental Ladder

Al Ries and Jack Trout, in their classic book, *Positioning, the Battle for Your Mind*, compare the way the human mind understands, organizes, and stores competitive products to the rungs of a stepladder. "To cope with our overcommunicated society, people have learned to rank products on mental ladders. In the rent-a-car field, for example, most people put Hertz on the top rung, Avis on the second rung, and National on the third."

The goal of a competitive presentation is to move your product or option to the top rung of this mental ladder so it becomes the top choice. Before you can prepare for a competitive presentation, you need to know who is ahead of you on that ladder. You will not move your audience to action by overcoming the wrong competitor. Here are some helpful questions to ask as you prepare for a competitive presentation:

→ What other suppliers are you currently using?
→ Are you talking to anyone else?
→ How many other organizations have you contacted?
→ How many other people are you considering?
→ Has your organization used any of the suppliers you are now considering in the past?
→ Are you considering an idea like the one I am proposing from anyone else?

Find Out What Your Competition Is Saying

When was the last time you checked your competition's Web site? When was the last time you asked audience members if they had heard a presentation similar to the one you just gave? The last time you had a friend pass on literature used by a competitor? When did you last call up a client friend after a competitor had made a presentation to them and asked what that competitor said? If it's been a long time since you have done any of the above, I have one more question for you.

When was the last time you lost business to a competitor and didn't see it coming?

The first step in getting competitive is understanding what your competition is actually doing. This takes extra work and asking the above questions is the best way to find out.

Says Herb Schiff, of Schiff & Associates, "If you don't know what your competitor is saying—verbally and in writing—you don't have a chance of doing any kind of competitive selling. You need to get their literature or hear what it is they're saying in actual presentations.

Over the years I have developed friends throughout my territory who call me when my competitors have just left their offices to tell me exactly what they said. As you start to gather this kind of intelligence, you will begin to understand how your competition thinks and reacts, and most importantly, what their weaknesses are."

Prepare to Differentiate

Before you can prove your proposal is better, you have to prove it is different. Typically, because you are involved with your presentation's content, you will see huge differences between what you are offering versus the competition. But to your audience, those differences may seem slight.

You need to plan a way to present your product or option so it seems *very* different. If you cannot first make the differences stick, then no competitive claims of being better will stick either. The following are several approaches.

Differentiate on the Details. There are always small differences even between very similar products or services. As your audience looks over your offering, there will be some parts they see as having little importance and others as having great importance. Where they find importance, more attention will be paid and small differences can seem huge.

If you discover that your audience has a passion for writing with green pens and your office supply store is the only store in your city that can supply enough green pens, this small point—insignificant to most other audiences—could be an important differentiator. The power to make your proposal seem very different can be found in the details.

Differentiate on Relationships. Myles McGrane, vice president of operations at the Jacob Javits Convention Center in New York City, shares a story where informal conversations chose the winning supplier. Recalls McGrane, "We had seen all the formal presentations, and looked at the financial proposals. At that point we felt we could not make a bad decision. The remaining suppliers were all industry leaders who were extremely interested in being a part of our project."

At random, McGrane and his team invited individuals from the suppliers' companies for informal walks around his facility. They would chat, get to know each other in a less formal, more personal way. On the walk, McGrane would ask the suppliers to react to relevant parts of his facility. The decision as to which supplier got the project was tipped by these ad hoc conversations.

The more similar in features and price your offering is to that of your competitors, the more likely your differentiator will be in relationships and service.

Differentiate on the Interface. My book on selling trends, *Selling 2.0,* caused quite a stir when it stated, "There are bigger differences between how you and your competition handle customers than there are between your products." Many technology trends are making products and services seem more similar. But new communication technologies have made the art of customer interfacing far more varied.

Often there are huge differences in how competing organizations interface with customers, other organizations, and their supply chain. If after-sale-service or ongoing contact is an important part of your proposal, the way your organization will interface can be a big differentiator. Say, "Our proposal includes 24/7 live telephone service, while our competitor just offers support though e-mail." Or, "Our service executives all come from the industry and have a minimum of five years' experience, the highest in the industry."

Translate Differences into Benefits. Often it is not enough to identify differences—you need to translate them into specific benefits your audience understands. Simply stated, help them understand, "What's in it for me?"

If your company makes pancake syrup that is 16 percent sweeter than your nearest competitor, just stating the statistic will be a big bore to restaurant owners. Instead, you could translate this statistic into a benefit specific to restaurant owners: Share a survey that shows how restaurant customers who were served breakfast with a sweeter pancake syrup thought their pancakes, French toast, and waffles all tasted much better. You could present the case that switching to your syrup would positively improve the experience of about half of their breakfast customers.

Develop a Competitive Approach

How will you best move your product or option to the top of the mental ladder that contains your competitors? Here are five competitive approaches from which to choose.

1. Be Comparative.

→ Is your IT solution cost effective? Compared to which others?
→ Is your budget comprehensive? Compared to who else's budget?
→ Is your action plan innovative? Compared to what?

The most common and easily accepted way to introduce competitive information into a presentation is to present it as comparative, not competitive. A comparative presentation lays out all the elements of your offering alongside those of all your competitors. It is important that your analysis include all your competitors, not just the ones ahead of you in the mind ladder. For the sake of maintaining credibility, it is important to be objective. I find that including at least one comparison where my product or option is not the best one always boosts credibility.

Graphically, you can make up PowerPoint slides with side-by-side lists of attributes. The number of slides you need will be determined by how many attributes are relevant for your offering. For complicated comparisons, I have used a series of slides, with each one making just one attribute comparison. Then I concluded with a summary slide listing all attribute comparisons together. I have also made much simpler comparisons where all attributes could be presented on a single slide. For example:

TRADE MAGAZINE ADVERTISING

COMPETITOR	CIRCULATION	EDITORIAL FOCUS	COST OF A PAGE OF AD
A	10,000	Focus on just marketing bats	$3,000
B	15,000	All aspects of bat business	$5,000
C	12,000	Focus on just raising bats	$4,000

I always find that audiences welcome all-inclusive, objective comparisons because they do part of the evaluative work for them.

2. Competitive Repositioning. While it is important for your product to be on the top rung of your audience's mental ladder, it is also important to be on the right ladder. When you reposition your product or your competitor's product, you not only rearrange the order your products take on the ladder, you rearrange the ladder itself.

Let's say you supply seafood to local restaurants and compete with local distributors, as well as national food distributors who supply many kinds of foods including seafood. If you were to make up a comparative chart (as in approach number 1) and put both local and national suppliers on it, you would not come out on top. But what if you described the ladder differently, and showed only local seafood suppliers on it? Then you could be on the top rung.

When you start rearranging these ladders, you can't just pick groups that conveniently eliminate competitors you don't want to talk about. You have to define a group in a way that makes sense to your audience. A group of all-local seafood suppliers makes sense, and by positioning your company among just them, you can look like the top pick.

My colleague Ann Belle Rosenberg uses a series of circles to position her publication against others in her market. One circle is labeled "video production magazines," another circle is labeled "broadcast magazines," and another labeled "audiovisual, or AV, magazines." Within each of these circles are listed the three or four magazines that serve each of those groups. The circles overlap in certain places, reflecting the overlap in magazine circulation. Ann Belle concludes that her publication is positioned on top of the list in the "video production magazine" circle.

Using this method she was once able to dissuade an advertiser from buying ad space in another publication by clearly demonstrating to him that the publication belonged in a different category than the one he initially thought. I heard the client say, "You know I never thought of it that way. I really should not advertise in that magazine, it's an AV magazine."

When you move a competitor to another ladder (or circle as in Rosenberg's case) you are, in essence, saying, "That may be a fine option but it is a different kind of option, and it may not be appropriate for you."

There are times you do not need to be the top rung on the ladder to succeed. If you know that your buying committee will select three suppliers out of a field of ten, you need only finish on one of the three top rungs. Here having a dialogue about which three companies top their choice list is critical.

Sometimes you can be number two on the ladder and get selected because people like to root for the underdog. In 1962, Avis was an unprofitable company with just eleven percent of the U.S. car rental business. Legendary adman Bill Bernbach recommended an improvement of Avis' customer service and an ad campaign that celebrated their status as the number two market underdog. Berbach's ad campaign invited travelers to use Avis with the slogan "We Try Harder." Within a year after Bernbach's campaign, Avis was profitable, and by 1966 Avis had tripled its market share to 35 percent.

3. Dramatize a Unique Benefit. In 1975, marketing wizard John Sculley, then-marketing chief at the soft drink division of PepsiCo, uncovered a disconnect among soda drinkers. When they were surveyed on which soft drink they preferred, most said, "Coke." But when they tasted Pepsi and Coke side by side in a blind taste test, many more preferred the sweeter taste of Pepsi.

Sculley dramatized this advantage by setting up blind taste tests in malls, shopping centers, and public locations where Pepsi representatives would present a table with two unmarked cups.

If the tasters were able to correctly identify which drink was Coke and which was Pepsi, they won a prize. This campaign, known as the "The Pepsi Challenge," dramatized Pepsi's advantage and won market share for Sculley's soft drink.

4. Get Them to Laugh at Competitors. Herb Schiff, of Schiff & Associates, uses the power of humor to win competitive advantage. Schiff's approach is to make fun of competitors, without appearing mean spirited or personal in any way, eventually getting his audience to laugh along with him.

Schiff starts by getting detailed intelligence on what his competition is actually saying in their presentations and literature. Says Schiff, "Once you know what your competitors are saying about themselves and about you, you will find there's always something they are saying that is just dead wrong. Find these things and go to work on them." Schiff then shares these misspeaks in a humorous way. He adds, "Regardless of what the competitors say, I never get angry and always appear to take it as a joke."

Once you make your competitors seem even slightly ridiculous, you begin to erode their credibility. According to Schiff, "As you continue to point out inconsistencies in a humorous way, if you can get an audience to agree that just one thing they say is completely ludicrous, the rest follows suit. Their credibility is destroyed, and from that point on there's nothing that competitor can present that's not going to be questioned."

5. Getting Competitive. There are times when you just will not win unless you get more aggressive than the approaches I've described so far. In a competitive, not comparative, presentation you compare your product or option directly to the competitor ahead of you on the audience's mental ladder. Your stated goal is to get your audience to choose yours over theirs. I advise caution with this more focused approach. If your audience sees you as "negative selling" and reacts badly, it will backfire.

But talking about your competition's negatives can be persuasive. Dr. L. Patrick Devlin, professor of Communication Studies at the University of Rhode Island, studies presidential campaigns and describes how this works: "There are many different ways people vote and only one of them is to vote for the candidate they want. Very often, people are motivated to vote against a candidate they don't like. By reinforcing another candidate's negatives, it's possible to motivate voters to support you by magnifying latent negative feelings about someone else."

Devlin advises that this approach is less effective in primary campaigns with a large number of candidates. Here, magnifying a negative may shift a vote away from a competitor but does not assure that you will get the vote with so many other choices. This approach works best in the final election, when it is down to just two main candidates, where shifting a vote away from one will likely move it to the other. If you are making a one-to-one, you-versus-them competitive presentation, this approach may be worth the risk.

Prepare the Audience for a Competitive Presentation

If members of your audience have personal relationships with your competitors, you could be doing yourself a lot of damage by attacking them directly. Here are some approaches to use before giving a competitive presentation.

Attack as a Victim. I once had a competitor send around a series of competitive "sell sheets" that highlighted the weaknesses of my offerings. Some were stronger than others, but none had a tremendous impact. But I collected them all and used them to create my own competitive presentation. I would begin by saying

> Misinformation is bad for everyone's business. As you may know, I have a competitor who has been highly critical of my offering. In the name of fighting misinformation, I would like to set the record straight about it.

I had copied the sell sheets into a PowerPoint presentation and assembled information that neutralized their claims, sheet by sheet. Then I turned the same microscopic lens on their offerings and showed that while they were good at slinging the mud at us, their own house was not in great shape.

The presentation had a devastating effect on my competitor. By sharing their own competitive materials and documenting how misleading they were, I was able to seriously compromise their credibility.

Get an Invitation. Competitive presentations are not for every audience. Before you jump into one, you need to get their permission to proceed. First, start with a comparative presentation. Then ask questions like, "Do these comparisons surprise you? Does this support what you've heard from other suppliers in the market? Has Competitor X shared this kind of information with you?"

Somehow you need to get them to talk about Competitor X and you are hoping for some inconsistencies to surface that would make it appropriate for you to "set the record straight" with a one-on-one comparison.

Lay Down a Challenge. I was once in a very competitive selling situation where it was clear that the buying committee was totally sold on my competitor. With my back against the wall, I laid down a challenge: "I understand how you have thought this through, and are thinking of going with another product, but what if I could prove to you that my option is better? I'd like to show you a detailed, head-to-head comparison before you proceed." My challenge was, in essence, an invitation to myself to give a competitive presentation.

Step by Step: The Presentation

First, Do No Harm

The sentiment in the line above is from the Hippocratic oath, taken by doctors as they begin their careers. This line also offers a sober warning when beginning a competitive presentation. There are times when making a competitive presentation will cause offense and do you more harm than good. You must constantly monitor your audience for negative reactions.

The first time you mention a competitor in your presentation, watch carefully for a reaction. If you may see skeptical looks that say, "Here we go again, another dope trying to put down a competitor," stop and take notice.

If I get any kind of negative reaction, I stop and immediately ask my audience for some feedback: "I see from your reaction that you're familiar with competitor X. Do you do business with him now?" Once I understand the audience's relationship with competitor X, I may alter my approach or drop the competitive presentation altogether.

Motivate Audience Involvement

With competitive presentations it is easy for an uninvolved audience to remain silent. No involvement usually means no traction. If you do all the talking, chances are you are not doing much persuading.

Your ultimate goal in a competitive presentation is to get your product or option chosen by moving it to the top rung of their mental ladder. Without audience feedback, you will never know where you are on that ladder or if you have made any progress toward moving up. Here are some ways to motivate that feedback.

Make It Fun. Some people like to talk about competitive rivalries. I had a client who just could not wait for me to visit so she could "dish the dirt" about my competitors. For audience members like this, approaching competitors as a big circus helps them share competitive gossip and information.

"It's to Your Advantage." If your audience trusts and respects your opinion, then your perspective on your competition would be beneficial for them to hear. Say, "If you better understand the people competing for your business it will help you get the most from all of us. I can help you better understand them if you share with me what my competition is saying."

"I'll Help You Do the Work." If you become known as the source for objective comparative information, people will be willing to share competitive information with you. In some cases you are doing their work for them, and a favor deserves a favor in return.

It's about the Dialogue

When the side-by-side specifics of competitors are put up on a PowerPoint screen, your hope is that they will prompt a detailed dialogue about your competitors that would be difficult to initiate any other way.

Then you can initiate discussion in areas you are concerned with. Say, "In this comparison we can see that Zonko Corporation has the most distributors in Rhode Island. Is that a big factor in how you will choose a distribution partner?"

Value-Shift Moments

I find that a lot of opportunity to change an audience's mind comes as you present the comparative charts. Before you begin your presentation, often a significant percentage of their understanding of how your competition stacks up is formed from gossip, rumor, and malicious misinformation spread by competitors. When you lay out all the comparative facts side by side up on the screen, for the first time your audience will be able to view all options together and to see how they interrelate within the competitive landscape.

When viewed together, they often see individual competitors in a different light. Suddenly, one will seem more competitive, another will seem less viable, or one will appear to be very similar to another. By seeing all the competitors together, very often your audience will shift the value they place on one to another. With your guidance, your product or option will rise to the top.

Closing

At the start of a competitive presentation, your audience may think a competitor has a better product or option, but if the presentation has been effective, your audience should now see you on top.

First you need to confirm that you are, in fact, on that top rung: "Is there a question in anyone's mind that our seafood supply company would be best for your needs?"

Then, assuming a positive confirmation, ask for a commitment: "Thank you for that confirmation. How soon can we start to do some business?"

14

The Presentation That Wins over a Hostile Audience

Indifference is harder to fight than hostility, and there is nothing that kills an agitation like having everybody admit that it is fundamentally right.—Crystal Eastman (author and ACLU cofounder; 1881–1928)

When an audience does not complain, it is a compliment, and when they do it is a compliment, too, if unaccompanied by violence.—Mark Twain (American humorist, writer, and lecturer; 1835–1910)

As Senator John F. Kennedy began his campaign for the U.S. presidency, his religion became an issue. Concerns were raised that Kennedy, potentially the first Catholic-American president, would take his lead on key issues from the Vatican.

On September 7, 1960, a coalition of 150 conservative Protestant clergymen, led by Rev. Dr. Norman Vincent Peale, issued a statement containing the "key question" of whether Kennedy could function independently of the Catholic Church, which "insists that he is duty-bound to admit to its direction."

The story made the front page of the *New York Times*. Two days later the group set up an office in Washington, D.C. to encourage similar meetings throughout the country. It was estimated that Kennedy could lose 1.5 million votes to the "religious issue" if it was not neutralized. In a tight election that was eventually decided by less than 120,000 popular votes, Kennedy had to act.

Kennedy caused quite a stir when he accepted an invitation to address this issue before the conservative Greater Houston Ministerial Association. His campaign staff, including his brother Robert Kennedy, unanimously advised against it, fearing their candidate would be fed to the lions. Texas Democrat Sam Rayburn told Kennedy, "They're mostly Republicans and they're out to get you."

The event was carried live on national television. Recognizing the potential for sparks to fly; the Rev. George Reck introduced Kennedy and then reminded his audience to "rely upon your sense for good order, proper respect for the nominee to the highest office of our land, and good Christian behavior generally."

Kennedy began by raising the level of the discussion by speaking, not about Catholics versus Protestants, but about the United States' national values that call for religious freedom: "I believe in an America where the separation of church and state is absolute—where no Catholic prelate would tell the President (should he be Catholic) how to act, and no Protestant minister would tell his parishioners for whom to vote... This is the kind of America I believe in—and this is the kind I fought for in the South Pacific, and the kind my brother died for in Europe...."

Then Kennedy went local with a reference to Texan sons sacrificed at the battle of the Alamo: "For side by side with Bowie and Crockett died Fuentes, and McCafferty, and Bailey, and Badillo, and Carey—but no one knows whether they were Catholics or not; for there was no religious test there."

Then Kennedy repositioned himself for his audience: "Contrary to common newspaper usage, I am not the Catholic candidate for president. I am the Democratic Party's candidate for president who happens also to be a Catholic. I do not speak for my Church on public matters—and the Church does not speak for me."

Near the end Kennedy offered a guarantee, pledging to resign the presidency if a time came when his religious beliefs and presidential responsibilities conflicted and he had to "either violate my conscience or the national interest."

Tough questions from the audience followed, but the session ended with laughter and enthusiastic applause. The next day the sponsoring association called Kennedy's address "the most complete, unequivocal and reassuring statement which could be expected of any person in his position."

The "religious issue" stopped dogging Kennedy, who went on to narrowly win the election by defeating California Senator Richard M. Nixon. So completely had the "religion issue" been turned around that on the morning of Kennedy's victory, Nixon was awakened by his six-year-old daughter who asked, "Daddy, why did people vote against you because of religion?"

HOW THIS WORKS

When a presentation is given to a potentially hostile audience, the stakes are raised. The anticipated conflict creates drama that adds importance and attracts a special kind of attention. The risks of failure are great but when these situations are turned into a win, it is the kind of event of which presentation legends are made.

Pitfalls

Thinking You Have Done Something Wrong Because Your Audience Is Angry

When you walk into a room with a hostile audience, it can be very intimidating. But very often, their anger is the result of anxiety, fear, or misunderstanding that has little to do with what you are offering or anything you have said. I once faced an audience who was very angry over a mixup by my company. But why anger? Similar organizations had reacted to similar mixups with much less antagonism. The answer lay deeper, in the emotional makeup and history of the audience.

Thinking You Will Never Sell an Angry Audience

Over the years I have noticed that many of my deepest client relationships began with very tough presentations. Audiences that react strongly to what you present, even with anger, are going to be more involved and passionate about your offerings. Often audiences that start out angry are the ones with the most potential. Anger comes from an audience's passion, not from their indifference, and passionate audiences always have more potential.

Step by Step: Preparation

Ask Yourself, "Is This about Concessions?"

Some audiences react in anger because they think there is an opportunity to gain concessions or extra attention. Concession-driven anger becomes apparent when the venting seems a prelude to negotiation. Audience members point out better pricing—or better something—from competitors, or shortcomings in your service that need extra attention, all implying that a concession makes sense. If the behavior seems calculated to put you on the defensive, it's probably being manufactured in the name of gaining a concession. If so, prepare for negotiations: Your audience is interested in what you are offering.

Prepare to Keep a Businesslike Manner Even When Provoked

Andy Rogers returned from World War II a decorated war hero, earning both a Silver and Bronz Star as well as a Purple Heart. What he did not realize then was that his most combative moments were possibly ahead of him while serving as chairman of his local school board.

Rogers and his neighbors had become alarmed when their new school district superintendent began hiring unqualified, political appointees. Fearing that the educational quality of their neighborhood schools was being traded for political gain, Rogers and several community members ran for election to the local school board and won enough seats to oust the corrupt superintendent. But the superintendent's supporters vowed to block the new board's vote. Protesters disrupted and ended the board's first monthly meeting without any business being conducted.

With police and security guards present, Rogers attempted to conduct the next few meetings. Amid protests, scuffles, and objects being thrown from the audience, the business of the school board began to move ahead. Rogers recalls, "I was always very businesslike and polite. I would read from a prepared agenda and I would call on people to speak, including the protesters." Rogers allowed everyone, including protesters, to voice their opinions but limited speaking time to three minutes each. When protesters went over their time limit, Rogers would politely turn off their microphone and proceed.

The 4:00 p.m. meeting at which they planned to vote to oust the superintendent was delayed by 20 minutes when protesters released half a dozen mice on the auditorium stage. After they were rounded up, the vote was again delayed several more times by noisy demonstrations. But Rogers's polite, businesslike calm kept the meeting moving forward. The vote that ousted the corrupt superintendent finally took place at 7:00 p.m. that night.

Stage the Room for Accommodation

Alan Gerson, a city councilman in New York City, once gave a proposal to bring together two feuding groups both occupying a city-sponsored building. Since Gerson was setting up the presentation, he could determine how the room would be set up and did so with a resolution in mind. He recalls, "The first thing I did was arrange the podium to have an impressive show of support for the proposal." Gerson arranged for people to be seated near the podium who represented both factions. Although there were deep disagreements between the leaders of the two groups, at the start of his presentation, a glance around the podium made them look like one big, happy family.

Step by Step: The Presentation

Let the Anger Vent

Dick Trask, vice president of marketing at Scala, once faced an audience with one relentlessly hostile individual. No matter what Trask said, this person would scowl, mutter under his breath, and raise his hand to challenge him whenever he tried to make a point.

Trask realized that unless he neutralized this hostile individual, his presentation would not go well. So he turned to the man and said, "It sounds like you have something you want to share with the audience. I was wondering if you could take a moment and share that with us now."

Recalls Trask, "He started off very hostile. But a minute or so into his talk, it just seemed like he couldn't keep up that level of anger; after all, he had the floor. After another minute his hostility faded and so did his enthusiasm for his diatribe. After another minute, it became painfully obvious that the audience was really there to listen to me, not him. Soon it became clear from looks from other audience members that it was time for him to sit down and shut up and time for me to resume my presentation."

Bottled up anger intensifies. Anger, once vented, diffuses. In the beginning it is best to let the anger out.

Listen for and Find the Deeper Source of Anger

Lee Iacocca, when he was CEO of Chrysler Corporation, was well prepared as he headed to Washington, D.C. to testify before congressional committees for the passage of a loan guarantee bill to help turn his company around. The congressional committee sessions were tough, as Iacocca recalled in his autobiography: "The questions came fast and furious, and they were always loaded. Staff members were constantly passing notes to the senators and congressmen, and I had to respond to everything off the cuff. It was murder."

Times were so bad at Chrysler that then-late-night talk show host Johnny Carson offered a definition of the meanest man in America as the one who calls up Chrysler and asks, "How's business?"

Wisconsin's Senator William Proxmire, chairman of the Senate Banking Committee, addressed Iacocca with skepticism: "You are now asking the government to risk $1.5 billion. If it fails, the taxpayer takes a painful bath. If it succeeds, you will be a famous success and be made very, very wealthy." Another Committee member commented, "The American people will not voluntarily invest in mismanagement."

Iacocca quickly established the fact that if Chrysler, then the tenth-largest corporation in America, went out of business, hundreds of thousands of jobs would disappear. He described his new management team, how he had reorganized his company, and the need to keep Chrysler competitive.

Eventually, the deeper fear that drove much of the anger surfaced. If Chrysler got a loan guarantee to avoid bankruptcy, then a precedent would be set and every company facing bankruptcy would have their hand out to Congress. But Iacocca was prepared.

His research uncovered the fact that loan guarantees were nothing new to the U.S. Congress and that there had been, in fact, $409 billion in similar assurances made to companies in the past. Iacocca countered the "precedent question" by responding, "We are setting no precedent. There are already $409 billion of loan guarantees on the books, so don't stop now, men. Go for $410 billion for Chrysler....There are 600,000 jobs involved here."

At the end of Iacocca's long testimony, his chief adversary, Senator William Proxmire, paid him a high compliment: "As you know, I am opposed to your request. But I have rarely heard a more eloquent, intelligent, well-informed witness than you have been today. You did a brilliant job, and we thank you. We are in your debt." Chrysler won enough votes to win passage of the loan guarantee bill. Despite his high praise for Iacocca's testimony, however, Senator Proxmire, true to his word, voted against it.

Anger is emotional, not logical. Very often as your audience vents anger they will not articulate a logical reason for it. But if you listen carefully for the feeling behind the behavior, the reason may become clear. Start responding to the feeling that drives the anger and you my get to the heart of the matter.

Encourage Venting Beyond the Anger

Once your audience has vented their anger, keep them talking. Ask questions about their concerns. Some audiences are surprised when I do this, expecting me to take my beating and then try to quickly change the subject. But by keeping the discussion going longer you can be assured that there are no other things they are upset over that will surface later. It is also a way to show extra concern.

After the anger is all out, it is time to react to what has been shared. You need to acknowledge the feelings that have been expressed and respond appropriately. If you or your organization made mistakes, apologies need to be made. If specific actions are required, see to those now.

Prove Yourself All Over Again

Ann Belle Rosenberg, marketing manager at Primedia Business, had been so successful at selling ad space for her magazine that her company asked her to take on another, less successful, publication. But as she began selling ads for this new magazine, she encountered unexpected hostility on a sales call at a company where she had always enjoyed a great relationship.

On a routine sales call to this company, she began by reviewing the current advertising program they had with her first publication. Then, she broke the news about her new assignment. Abruptly the atmosphere in the room turned negative. Several committee members looked shocked, as if Rosenberg had betrayed them. One committee member involuntarily blurted out, "No, Ann Belle, you can't do this to us!" Another looked squarely at her and asked if she had lost her mind. For the first few minutes, the room was in chaos. Finally, the committee chair restored order by saying, "Look, I'm sure Ann Belle has her reasons for this." Then she faced Rosenberg and said, "Ann Belle, before you tell us about this new magazine of yours, I want you to know this is not personal, but we are never, ever, advertising in that magazine."

Rosenberg swallowed hard and began her presentation. Despite her long-standing relationship, they grilled her like they had just met her for the first time. Their anger drove them to ask questions hard and fast. But the more Rosenberg responded, the more the committee realized that they did not really know this publication. After a number of "Oh, I didn't realize that" moments, Rosenberg's audience began to warm.

Finally, the committee chair smiled at her and said, "For the past five years, it's been a standing joke around here that we would never advertise in your new magazine. The truth is, we couldn't stand the salesperson before you. Years ago, he came in here and was so abrasive and condescending that we never wanted to see him again. But he hounded us relentlessly. After we had all been harassed enough we agreed we would never advertise with him, hoping he would leave us alone. But I now see that a lot has changed over the years when we were out of the loop. Ann Belle, we're glad you explained these things to us today." Rosenberg got an ad contract a month later.

Despite her long-standing relationship with this group, Rosenberg had to prove herself all over again, and only after she had done so did they share the deeper reason for their initial anger.

Move to Higher Ground. Assuming that whatever proposal you put on the playing field will be quickly challenged, take the first few minutes to raise the entire playing field to a higher level. Raising the level of the argument always favors the underdog, and doing this challenges your audience to evaluate what you say at a higher level.

As a candidate John F. Kennedy, wishing to avoid a divisive discussion of Catholic-versus-Protestant beliefs, raised the level of the argument to focus on values of religious freedom assured by the U.S. Constitution.

Some other examples:

1. *We all need to please someone more important (customers, shareholders, voters, top management, etc.).* "What's more

important than my opinion or yours is how this will play to your organization's customers."

2. *To get the best (ideas, proposals) you need to hear everyone out.* "I understand you have a relationship with one of my competitors, but to get the best from all of your potential suppliers it is to your advantage to hear us all out so you can make the best decisions."

Recognizing the Transitional Moment

If you are successful in diffusing the anger and go on to begin stating your case, there will come a transitional moment where the mood in the room begins to shift. If it took all your allotted presentation time to get this far, call it "a win" and ask for another appointment. But if you reach this point early in your session I say go back and turn this into a sale. There is no better time to do this. You will often find a very receptive audience. Here's why:

1. *There is an air of honesty.* After a lot of venting the masks are off and you will get more honest feedback that will help you advance your proposal.

2. *Nothing builds credibility like successfully making your way through a brutal session.* Assuming a successful resolution, you will have earned fresh respect.

3. *If the anger was caused by miscommunication on the audience side, there will be some guilt working in your favor.*

Use the Emotion to Fuel Engagement

As your audience passes the "transition point" and seems ready to listen to what you have to say, ironically this is the time to stop talking. It is time to get them to do the talking... again.

Most audiences become angry because they feel you do not understand them. Your audience may feel disappointment, betrayal, offense, or shock at the behavior of you or your organization, but they felt you understood them would not be yelling.

Stop and get them to talk about their situation in detail. Shut up and listen. I find that anger will drive an audience to share far more than would normally be open to you. Often in the deeper sharing comes deeper opportunity for understanding and eventually ways to reshape your proposal.

Closing

When you present to a hostile audience, if you can successfully channel the passion of the moment into a more intense dialogue, you can turn a potentially disadvantageous situation into an extremely persuasive presentation.

However, that's a best-case scenario. In reality the outcome isn't always this "picture perfect." Your degree of success in turning around the hostility will determine what approach you should take to close. Whether the situation worked out as a big win, a loss, or just a draw, there is a way to deal with it.

Here are three possible outcomes and ways to close with each.

A Big Win

Here, you were able to neutralize the hostility and channel the increased energy in the room into a greater understanding overall and then move back into presentation mode to share a modified proposal.

In this case you can use "postproblem bonding" to move toward a commitment. After a presenter and audience have worked through a misunderstanding serious enough to cause open hostility, there is usually a sense of mutual accomplishment.

Typically in working out your differences, a greater understanding on both sides results, which should allow you to modify your proposal to be more on target for your audience's needs. Your proposal is still going to have to stand on its own merit, and you are still going to have to present and explain it in a way that wins acceptance. But as you head to the close I find you can often seal the deal by bringing forward the mutual feeling of understanding that has emerged.

I once closed a situation like this by saying,

> An hour ago you all thought I was crazy [some laughter]. But now I feel we have come together and are all on the same page. [Pause a beat for the nice moment]. Sometimes it takes extraordinary circumstances to reach an extraordinary understanding, and that is what we have done today. We can all feel proud of how we have moved past our differences and come together to shape this proposal. Is this something on which we can move forward?

A Loss

Here, you went before the hostile audience knowing the risks. You held your own but ran out of time and were not able to shift back into presentation/selling mode to share a proposal. Hopefully, you've earned your audience's respect and established a relationship beach head.

You cannot ask for a commitment to a proposal you never had a chance to present, but you can capitalize on your new relationship by asking for another time to come in and present it.

Say, "I'm glad we had a chance to work though our differences this morning. I now have a much better understanding of your needs and feel I could put together a proposal that you will find compelling. May I come back and share these ideas with you?"

A Draw

Here, your presentation went okay, but it wasn't terrific. You were able to neutralize your audience's anger and just barely started presenting your product or option. What you need is the opportunity to come back and finish the job. Summarize the points you made during your dialogue, paying particular attention to the points where your audience was especially interested in what you were saying—their hot buttons.

> During the time we spent together I feel we've reached a greater understanding of one another. I noticed that you're especially interested in several areas of my presentation, namely A, B, and C. I'd like the opportunity to come back and share with you some ideas I have about those. Is there a time when we can all sit down together?

Before you leave, try to get everyone to pull out their calendars and fix a date.

Appendix A

The "Eyes Rules"

The 1987 documentary television series *Eyes on the Prize* chronicled the civil rights movement and won huge audiences for PBS as well as many awards for the small Boston film company that produced it, called "Blackside."

Stanford University history professor Clayborne Carson, editor of Martin Luther King Jr.'s papers, called *Eyes on the Prize* "the principal film account of the most important American social justice movement of the twentieth century."

I worked as a producer on other programs at Blackside while *Eyes* was being produced there. Steve Fayer who served as series writer for *Eyes*—and won a national Emmy for his script, "Mississippi: Is This America?"—was also script supervisor for most of the programs I produced there.

Fayer, a self-taught writer who had never been to film school or worked on a national PBS series before *Eyes*, describes it as an extraordinary learning experience. After the initial telecast, he decided to codify the *Eyes on the Prize* approach—to create a common film vocabulary that could be shared with other professionals on future projects. Around Blackside, the "Eyes Rules" instantly became a part of the company culture, and we referred to them often, even when working on other productions.

The Eyes Rules are as relevant today as they were back in the 1980s when Fayer created them as a guide for keeping content and stories credible, relevant, and on point for any kind of script development.

They are reproduced here with Steve Fayer's permission.

When artists, intentionally or not, distort the known facts to get an effect, either political or commercial, they are on the wrong side of the line between poetic truth and historical falsification.

Artists who present as fact things that never happened, who refuse to allow the truth to interfere with a good story, are betraying their art and history as well.—Richard Bernstein ("Can Movies Teach History?" New York Times, November 26, 1989)

Eyes-Style Rules

1. Use narration only to tell us something we do not see in the frame or to provide context that the audience cannot know or create for itself.

2. Avoid using adjectives and adverbs—particularly judgmental ones.

3. Don't talk back to a picture or carry on a conversation with it when writing narration.

4. Let the audience draw its own conclusions.

5. Follow basic dramatic structure: three acts. First, set up forces in opposition—(put your) man up the tree, and start throwing stones at him. Second act—in so much trouble you wonder how he'll ever get out of this mess. Third act—for better or worse, get him down out of the tree.

6. Remember, we are not telling a complete history, or attempting to. We are telling stories from the history. And stories do not work very well without dramatic structure.

7. Tell the truth. When there is more than one truth, tell both of them.

8. Include testimony against interest to make your story legitimate and build audience confidence in you. Meaning: Let the spokespeople for the other side of the issue be heard, no matter how wrong-headed you feel they are.

9. Avoid the passive voice whenever possible. Make most sentences active to keep the story moving.

10. "Nothing beats a great talking head"—Jon Else. Stories will play in people's minds like great radio if you have a great storyteller. You *see it* in your head.

11. Do not mess with "pieces of the true cross," in interviews or archival footage. ("Pieces of true cross" is Blackside internal shorthand for important and hard-to-find documentary footage. If footage is flawed in some way, e.g., audience hears

sound rolling and coming up to speed, do not attempt to pretty up the reality. Accept it. Use it.)

12. Do not sandbag people, either in present-day interviews or archival footage. (Avoid using narration to set up and then contradict a talking head. At Blackside, narration's job is to steer the film, not judge the witnesses.)

13. Be careful with back story (exposition). Audiences watch movies for movement, to learn what's going to happen next, not necessarily to learn, period. Even PBS audiences.

14. Avoid opening with long narrative passages that tell us what this is all about. Footage, archival or new interview, usually works better.

15. Avoid words that end in *-ing* or *-ion*. The first signals that action has slowed down; the second that you are going intellectual on us.

16. Finally, question commonly accepted opinions about people and events before making them your own. You know you are in trouble when you begin to defend a line of narration with "Everybody knows that ..."

Appendix B

Picking the Right Strategy, by the Numbers

Which of the 14 persuasive strategies you use for your next presentation will depend on your audience, your message, and your situation. While I can't predict your specifics, I can offer a "best-practice" guide as to how often these strategies are used through a survey done exclusively for this book.

The survey was conducted on the readers of *Presentations* magazine, a publication written for people who use presentations professionally. The following 10 charts are based on 2,206 useable responses from magazine readers.

Chart 1: Strategies Used Most Often

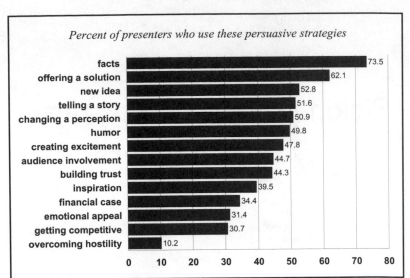

Percent of presenters who use these persuasive strategies

Strategy	Percent
facts	73.5
offering a solution	62.1
new idea	52.8
telling a story	51.6
changing a perception	50.9
humor	49.8
creating excitement	47.8
audience involvement	44.7
building trust	44.3
inspiration	39.5
financial case	34.4
emotional appeal	31.4
getting competitive	30.7
overcoming hostility	10.2

It should be no surprise that persuading with facts is the most commonly used strategy, as it is hard to lay out a persuasive case without them. But consider that every other strategy, except "overcoming hostility," is also very frequently used.

Suggestions and comments:

→ Presenters in this survey checked off an average of six strategies that they use. Do you want to give yourself an edge on your competition? Master them all.

→ I am highly suspicious of the low score that "emotional appeal" received, with fewer than one-third of presenters saying they use it to persuade. From my days working with Harvey Research, I know that when you survey salespeople they tend to downplay the emotional approaches they use. While this survey targets all executives giving presentations I believe the same psycology is in play. Every presentation has an emotional component, whether or not it is acknowledged consciously by the presenter.

The great Brian Tracy wrote in *Advanced Selling Strategies*: "All buying decisions are emotional because people are completely emotional in everything they say and do…They usually make their decisions quickly, even instantaneously, and then spend a good deal of time rationalizing and justifying why they have decided to act in a certain way."

Chart 2: Strategies Most Persuasive

*Percent of presenters who pick one of these these strategies as **the one** most persuasive strategy*

facts	15.5
offering a solution	15.2
audience involvement	13.9
telling a story	7.5
building trust	7.2
financial case	7
creating excitement	5.9
changing a perception	5.8
inspiration	5.2
new idea	4.4
emotional appeal	4.3
humor	4.1
getting competitive	3.1
overcoming hostility	0.5

All the persuasive strategies are used frequently, but this question asks presenters to pick *the one* strategy they believe is most persuasive. Using facts, offering a solution, and gaining audience involvement were the top picks by far.

Suggestions and comments:

→ Many presentations are combinations of the 14 persuasive strategies. You may start within a humorous story, continue by getting your audience excited about past accomplishments of your organization, and then present a solution you want them to accept.

→ As you plan your next presentation, remember the top three. Ask yourself:
"Are my facts straight?"
"Am I offering a solution?"
"Do I have an audience involvement strategy?"
You might want to look at Chapters 1, 7, and 11 again.

→ As to the question of an audience involvement strategy, on this chart we see that "audience involvement" is one of the most persuasive strategies by far. But if we go back to the first chart of this survey, we see that only 44.7 percent of presenters actually use this approach to plan ahead and think how they will engage their audience. Ouch! For a majority of presenters, audience involvement "just happens" without a conscious plan or strategy.

Chart 3: Most Persuasive Strategies
Ranked in Eight Industries

Presenters in eight industries rank the top five persuasive strategies as "most persuasive"

COMMUNICATIONS

1. offering a solution
2. facts
3. audience involvement
4. telling a story
5. emotional appeal

EDUCATION

1. audience involvement
2. facts
3. offering a solution
4. creating excitement
5. inspiration

ENGINEERING

1. offering a solution
2. facts
3. audience involvement
4. financial case
5. inspiration

FINANCIAL

1. audience involvement
2. offering a solution
3. financial case
4. facts
5. emotional appeal

HI TECH

1. offering a solution
2. facts
3. building trust
4. audience involvement
5. financial case

MANUFACTURING

1. facts
2. offering a solution
3. financial case
4. audience involvement
5. building trust

MEDICAL

1. facts
2. audience involvement
3. offering a solution
4. telling a story
5. changing a perception

PROFESSIONAL SERVICES

1. offering a solution
2. audience involvement
3. building trust
4. facts
5. telling a story

The whole premise of this book is that there is no "best and only" way to persuade every audience. Here is proof positive. In the financial and education industries, presenters rank getting "audiences involvement" as the most persuasive strategy. But presenters in the medical and manufacturing fields rank "laying out the facts" as the top persuasive strategy. In engineering, high-tech, communications, and professional services, the top strategy is "offering a solution."

Suggestions and comments:

→ As you plan your next presentation, consider the top five strategies for the industry most similar to the one to which you will present.

Chart 4: Funniest Presenters

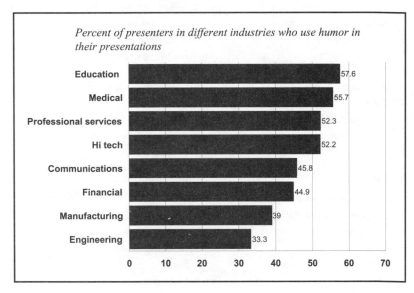

Percent of presenters in different industries who use humor in their presentations

Industry	Percent
Education	57.6
Medical	55.7
Professional services	52.3
Hi tech	52.2
Communications	45.8
Financial	44.9
Manufacturing	39
Engineering	33.3

Are teachers and doctors the funniest presenters? Are manufacturers and engineers the most serious?

Very likely. Presenters from the education and medical fields use the most humor in their presentations; presenters from manufacturing and engineering use less humor.

Chart 5: Most Competitive Presenters

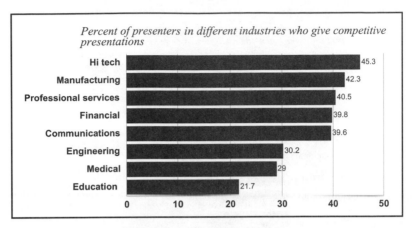

High-tech and manufacturing presenters use competitive presentations most often. Presenters in medical and educational industries use competitive presentations least often.

Chart 6: Most Imaginative Presenters

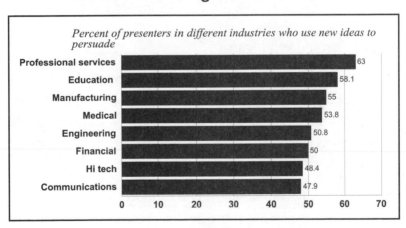

Use of new ideas to persuade is common in all industries measured. But people involved in professional services use more new ideas to persuade, and presenters from communications industries use the least.

Chart 7: Most Hostile Audiences

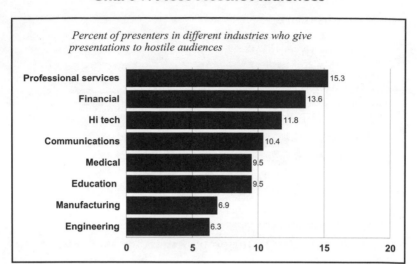

Percent of presenters in different industries who give presentations to hostile audiences

Professional services	15.3
Financial	13.6
Hi tech	11.8
Communications	10.4
Medical	9.5
Education	9.5
Manufacturing	6.9
Engineering	6.3

Professional and financial services offer presenters the most potentially hostile audiences, with 15.3 percent of professional services presenters saying they encounter them. Manufacturing and engineering presenters encounter the least number of hostile audiences.

Suggestions and comments:

→ Research done for my book *Tough Calls* proved that, on sales calls, hostility and anger come to the surface most often when more personal outcomes are at stake. It is no surprise that the industries where the interaction is more personal are the ones where hostile audiences are most frequent.

→ You might be wondering why I included "overcoming hostility" as a persuasive strategy. It is the least frequently used persuasive strategy, with only about 10 percent of presenters saying they use this approach. But this strategy is a confidence builder. It shows you that even if your audience becomes enraged, you can still come out a winner. It may be the least common strategy, but it is a unique situation that requires its own approaches.

→ I also find that the most hostile presentations I encounter often result in the greatest gain, most quickly. The biggest loss while presenting is when there is no hostility, anger, or communication of any kind. First, there's a quick glance at the watch by the committee chairperson, followed by a polite request to "wrap this up in the next five minutes," followed by no returned phone calls.

A hostile audience that is willing to engage you and express their rage, frustration, and anger is the biggest prize a master presenter can find. If you know how to turn an angry audience around, it is a gift in disguise.

Chart 8: Ways to Begin a Presentation

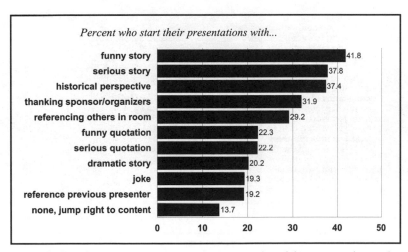

Percent who start their presentations with...

	Percent
funny story	41.8
serious story	37.8
historical perspective	37.4
thanking sponsor/organizers	31.9
referencing others in room	29.2
funny quotation	22.3
serious quotation	22.2
dramatic story	20.2
joke	19.3
reference previous presenter	19.2
none, jump right to content	13.7

The cliché that says every presentation should start with a joke should be retired. Stories, both funny and serious, are the preferred way to begin a persuasive presentation.

Only about 14 percent of presenters say they jump right into their content without some kind of opening.

→ Introductions that are unrelated to the content or presenters are a missed opportunity. Bill Bison, publisher of *Pensions & Investments,* said it best: "Giving a presentation—it starts with your underwear. If you don't have the willingness to throw yourself in and invest yourself completely, you're never going to be very good."

Bison was right. From the start, you need a total commitment. The first thing you say will make an impression that will stay with your audience.

Chart 9: Building Trust

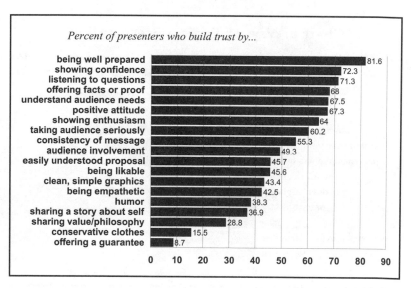

Percent of presenters who build trust by...

being well prepared	81.6
showing confidence	72.3
listening to questions	71.3
offering facts or proof	68
understand audience needs	67.5
positive attitude	67.3
showing enthusiasm	64
taking audience seriously	60.2
consistency of message	55.3
audience involvement	49.3
easily understood proposal	45.7
being likable	45.6
clean, simple graphics	43.4
being empathetic	42.5
humor	38.3
sharing a story about self	36.9
sharing value/philosophy	28.8
conservative clothes	15.5
offering a guarantee	8.7

The three most common ways presenters build audience trust are: being well prepared, showing confidence, and listening to audience questions.

Chart 10: Biggest Trust Builders

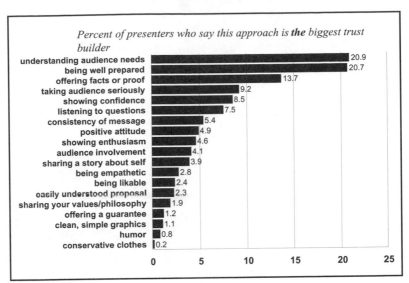

*Percent of presenters who say this approach is **the** biggest trust builder*

understanding audience needs	20.9
being well prepared	20.7
offering facts or proof	13.7
taking audience seriously	9.2
showing confidence	8.5
listening to questions	7.5
consistency of message	5.4
positive attitude	4.9
showing enthusiasm	4.6
audience involvement	4.1
sharing a story about self	3.9
being empathetic	2.8
being likable	2.4
easily understood proposal	2.3
sharing your values/philosophy	1.9
offering a guarantee	1.2
clean, simple graphics	1.1
humor	0.8
conservative clothes	0.2

While there are many ways presenters build trust, when presenters were asked to pick the *one* most effective trust builder, three approaches stood above the rest: understanding audience needs, being well prepared, and offering facts or proof.

→ Research from my book *Selling 2.0* shows that trust is not as easily earned on the superficial level as many believe. It takes effort and work to really understand an audience, prepare well, and research relevant facts and proof.

Approaches that require less "work," such as showing confidence, listening to questions, and being likeable, are easier to do but don't demonstrate through effort that you are trustworthy.

Earning audience trust is simple. They want to know that you are *working* for it.

For more results from the survey visit my Web site at www.JoshGordon.com.

Appendix C

Gender and Political Affiliation Contrast Study

You can learn about yourself as a persuasive presenter by considering which strategies and trust-building approaches you choose, and by which public figures you see as being "most persuasive." The following survey compared these against gender and political party. By how others choose we challenge ourselves to try new approaches.

This survey was conducted for this book over the readers of *SellingPower* magazine's Presentations Newsletter (free subscription at www.SellingPower.com) and is the result of 408 useable responses.

Top Five Persuasive Strategies by Gender

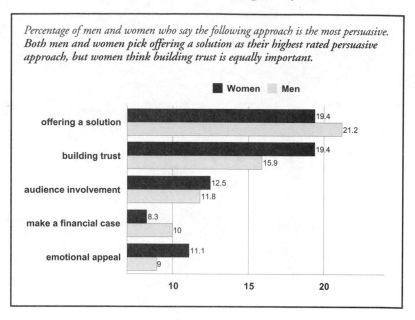

Percentage of men and women who say the following approach is the most persuasive. Both men and women pick offering a solution as their highest rated persuasive approach, but women think building trust is equally important.

Top Six Ways to Build Trust by Gender

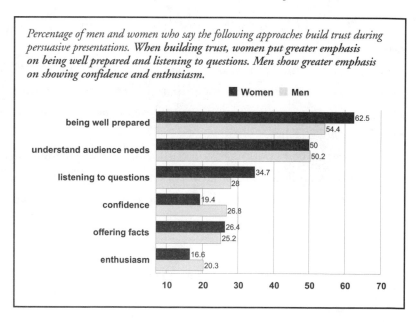

Percentage of men and women who say the following approaches build trust during persuasive presentations. When building trust, women put greater emphasis on being well prepared and listening to questions. Men show greater emphasis on showing confidence and enthusiasm.

Top Five Most Persuasive Presenters of Our Time by Gender

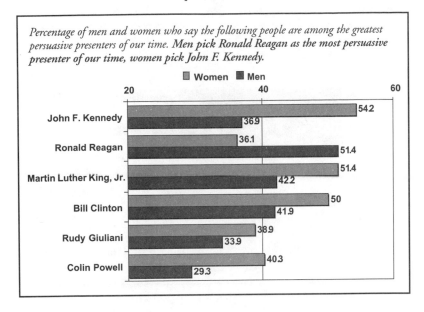

Percentage of men and women who say the following people are among the greatest persuasive presenters of our time. Men pick Ronald Reagan as the most persuasive presenter of our time, women pick John F. Kennedy.

Use Humor in Persuasive Presentations

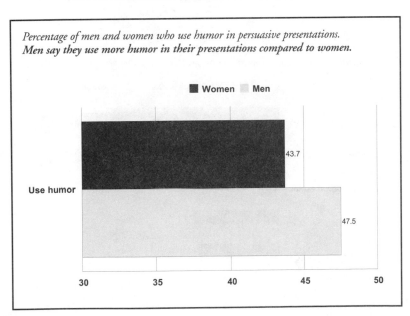

Percentage of men and women who use humor in persuasive presentations. Men say they use more humor in their presentations compared to women.

Use of Stories in Persuasive Presentations

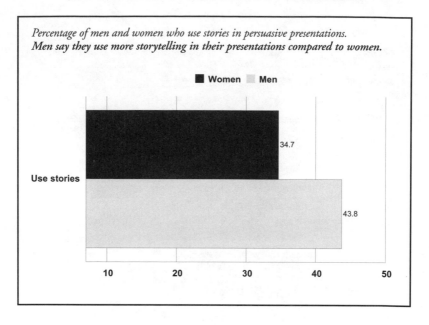

Percentage of men and women who use stories in persuasive presentations.
Men say they use more storytelling in their presentations compared to women.

Top Five Persuasive Strategies by Political Party

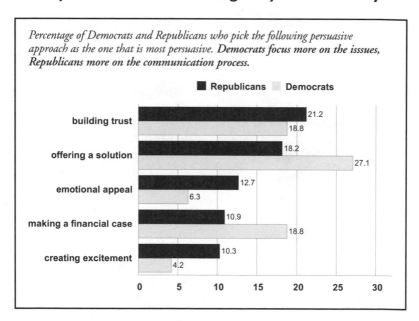

Percentage of Democrats and Republicans who pick the following persuasive
approach as the one that is most persuasive. **Democrats focus more on the issues,**
Republicans more on the communication process.

Top Five Trust-Building Strategies by Political Party

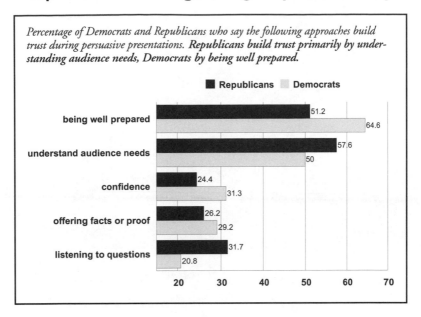

*Percentage of Democrats and Republicans who say the following approaches build trust during persuasive presentations. **Republicans build trust primarily by understanding audience needs, Democrats by being well prepared.***

Top Five Most Persuasive Presenters of Our Time by Political Party

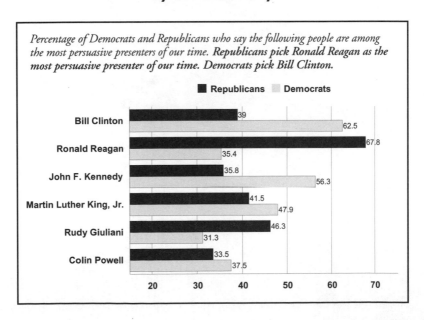

*Percentage of Democrats and Republicans who say the following people are among the most persuasive presenters of our time. **Republicans pick Ronald Reagan as the most persuasive presenter of our time. Democrats pick Bill Clinton.***

Index

Abernathy, Ralph, 70
Abstract thinking, 56
Academy Awards (2005), 25
Accountants, 199
Activities, 8
Adams, Joey, 92
Adapt the idea/give it away, 66–67
Adjectives, 238
Adverbs, 238
Ailes, Roger, 78
Allen, Woody, 43
Andersen Worldwide, 112
Anecdotal evidence, 111
Angell, Norman, 99
Anger. *See* Hostile audience
Anxiety, 75
Archambault, Carolyn, 122, 131
Arendt, Hannah, 35
Art of Selling, The (Goddard), 14
Ash, Mary Kay, 17
Asimov, Isaac, 171
Assumptions, 177–178
Attention grab, 61–62
Attributes, 145–146
Audience
    business presentation, 188–190
    decision-making process, 115–116
    feedback, 49–50
    hierarchy, 152–153
    hostile, 221–235. *See also* Hostile
      audience
    involvement. *See* Audience involve-
      ment
    language, 164–165

    negative reactions, 218
    passions, 21–22, 28–30
    risk aversion, 60–61, 158
Audience detective, 11–12
Audience involvement, 1–15, 244
    activities, 8
    audience detective, 11–12
    closing, 14–15
    ego, 9–10
    emotion, 6–7
    entertainment, 10–11
    graphics /charts, 8–9
    Iacocca effect, 13–14
    pacing, 12–13
    pitfalls, 4
    preparation, 4–11
    presentation, 11–15
    problem solving, 7–8
    relevancy, 5–6
    room setup, 11
    spontaneity, 10
Audubon Society, 149
Austin, Emory, 38, 48
Author. *See* Gordon, Josh
Avis Rent A Car, 214

Baby steps, 63–64
Back story (exposition), 240
Banking, 198
Beach ball, 8
Bean counters, 199
Beckley, Jim, 191
Bernbach, William, 69, 214
Bernstein, Richard, 238

Bishop, Cameron, 26, 117
Bison, Bill, 250
Blackside, 237
Blair, Tony, 102
Bloch, Ann, 41–42
Blodget, Henry, 194–195
Bodybuilding, 128
Boies, David, 203
Bombeck, Erma, 100
Borge, Victor, 83
Bottom-line approach, 191–192
Breakthrough technologies, 198
Brown, Dawn, 147–148
Build sequence, 182–183
Building trust. See Trust-building presentation
Businesslike manner, 225–226
Bush, George H. W., 156
Butts, Mike, 113

Calm to storm formula, 20
Carson, Clayborne, 237
Carson, Johnny, 91, 228
Chambers, John, 29
Change direction, 80–81
Changing a perception, 137–154
    attributes, 145–146
    audience hierarchy, 152–153
    closing, 153–154
    confirmation, 151–152
    fun, 148–149
    "it's my fault," 150–151
    offer something new, 142–144
    perception underlying attitude, 142
    permission to change, 150–151
    pitfalls, 140–141
    preparation, 141–149
    presentation, 150–154
    pro-change statement, 150
    redefine process of evaluation,
        144–145
    share new "standard," 147

    stories, 147–148
    what attitude to change?, 141
Charts, 8–9
"Checkers speech" (Nixon), 145
Christie, Agatha, 155
Chrysler Building, 18
Cisco Systems, 29
Civil Rights Act of 1964, 71
Clarke, Arthur C., 53
Clay, Henry, 203
"Clicks," 30–32
Clinton, Bill, 5, 13-14, 36–37, 156,
    255, 257
Clinton, Michael, 178–179
Clues to audience decision-making
    process, 115–116
Cocks, Sir Barnett, 53
Comedy. See Humorous presentation
Commodore Hotel, 18–19
Communications industry, 245–248
Compaq Computer, 62
Comparisons, 211–212, 219
Competitive presentation, 203–220
    attack as a victim, 216–217
    closing, 220
    comparisons, 211–212, 219
    competitive repositioning, 213–214
    differentiate, 209–211
    fun, 219
    get an invitation, 218
    how often used, 247
    humor, 215
    lay down a challenge, 217–218
    mental ladder, 207–208
    motivate audience involvement,
        218–219
    negative reactions, 218
    negative selling, 216
    overt attack on competitor, 206
    pitfalls, 206–207
    preparation, 207–218
    presentation, 218–220

side-by-side comparisons, 212, 219
unique benefit, 214–215
value-shift moments, 220
what is competition saying, 208–209
Competitive repositioning, 213–214
Concerns/objections, 65
Concession-driven anger, 225
Confirmation, 151–152
Consistency, 199–200
Context, 175, 176, 183
Courting Justice (Boies), 203
Cowley, Rick, 148–149
Crain's New York Business, 193
Creating excitement, 17–33
    audience's passions, 21–22, 28–30
    "clicks," 30–32
    close, 32–33
    early converts, 26
    enthusiasm building, 26–28
    hidden powder kegs, 28
    kickers (surprises), 22–24
    next level, 30–32
    pacing, 24–26
    pitfalls, 19–20
    preparation, 21–26
    presentation, 26–33
    visualize the result, 32–33
Crisis point, 41–42

da Vinci, Leonardo, 137
Davis, Bette, 167
Davis, Mark, 97
Dean, Richard, 36–37
Dell Computer, 55
Deukmejian, George, 86
Devlin, L. Patrick, 216
Diana, Princess, 100–102, 107, 115
Dickson, Jim, 95, 191–192
Differentiate, 209–211
Digital Research, 173
Disney, Roy, 2–3, 198–199
Disney, Walt, 2, 3

Disney Company, 2–3, 198
"Disneyland Story," 3
Dole, Bob 54
Dot-com bubble, 194
Doubt, 131
Downes, Donna, 164
Dramatic structure, 48–49, 239
Dramatize key facts, 111–113
Dress (attire), 164
Dull words, 43
Dynamic leaders, 198

Early converts, 26
Eastman, Crystal, 221
Economic decision-makers, 199–200
Education industry, 245–248
Edwards, John, 79
Ego, 9–10
Ego boost, 75
Einstein, Albert, 83, 174
Eisenhower, Dwight D., 144, 145
Emerson, Ralph Waldo, 17
Emotion, 243. *See also* Emotional appeal
    audience involvement, 6–7
    financial presentation, 197–198
    hostile audience, 232–233
Emotional appeal, 69–82
    align and yourself with message,
        76–77
    change direction, 80–81
    closing, 81–82
    emotional bounce, 79–80
    emotional honesty, 75–76
    emotional inventory, 73
    emotional investments, 77–78
    graphics, 77
    pitfalls, 71–72
    preparation, 72–77
    present from the heart, 78–79
    presentation, 77–82
    storyboard, 73–74
    what emotions?, 74–75

Emotional bounce, 79–80
Emotional honesty, 75–76
Emotional inventory, 73
Emotional investments, 77–78
Emotional logic card, 114
Endicott, Jim, 4–5, 8
Engineering industry, 245–248
Enron, 112
Entertainment, 10–11. *See also* Fun;
    Humor
Enthusiasm building, 26–28
Entitlement devil, 167
"Everybody know that...", 240
Everyday evangelism, 128
Exaggeration, 47
Examples, 132
Excitement. *See* Creating excitement
Expert, 111
Exposition (back story), 240
Eyes on the Prize, 48, 237–238
Eyes-style rules, 238–240

Facts. *See* Laying out the facts
Familiarity, 160
Faustman, Denise, 120
Fayer, Steve, 41, 48–49, 161, 237–238
Fear, 193–194
Female-male differences, 253–256
Financial community report, 111
Financial hook, 193–195
Financial industry, 245–248
Financial predictions, 196
Financial presentation, 185–201
    audience business model, 188–190
    bottom-line approach, 191–192
    closing, 200–201
    consistency, 199–200
    dynamic nature of numbers, 197
    economic decision-makers, 199–200
    emotion, 197–198
    fear, 193–194
    financial hook, 193–195

    find "the number," 191
    follow-up survey, 193
    greed, 193–194
    help them find the money, 211
    measures something
        nonfinancial/valuable, 192
    money timeline, 200–211
    pitfalls, 187–188
    preparation, 188–197
    presentation, 197–201
    storytelling, 195–197
    summary slide, 201
Financial story, 195–197
First impression, 163–164
Flat tax, 54
Follow-up survey, 193
Forbes, Malcolm, 171,
Forbes, Steve, 54, 57, 61
Ford, Henry, 161
Four Trials (Edwards), 79
Franklin, Benjamin, 1
Fun, 148–149, 219
Funniest presenters, 246

Galbraith, John Kenneth, 141, 185
Galford, Rob, 163, 167–168
Gamble, Doug, 84, 86, 95
Garfield, Bob, 156
Gates, Bill, 172–173
Gender differences, 253–256
General Motors (GM), 63
Gerson, Alan, 124, 226–227
Giuliani, Rudy, 78, 255, 257
Gleeson, Brad, 5
Goddard, F. B., 14
Goldwyn, Samuel, 53
Goodship, Strath, 195–196
Gordon, Josh
    books, 270
    company, 271–274
    contact information, 274
    historical overview, 269–270

Web site, 274
Gordon, Jenny, 145
Gordon, Laura, 13, 44-46
Gordon, Lynn, 7–8, 272
Gordon Communication Strategies,
    271–274
Grand Hyatt Hotel, 19
Graphics
    audience involvement, 8–9
    emotional appeal, 77
Great American Depression, The (Fayer),
    41
Greed, 193–194
Gschwandtner, Gerhard, vii, 77, 78, 167
Guarantee, 163

Hani, Chris, 138
Help people, 128
Herbert, Milt, 24, 29–30
Hicks, Robert E., 69
Hidden powder kegs, 28
High ground, 231–232
High tech industry, 245–248
Hill, Napoleon, 1
Hitchcock effect, 42
Hoff, Lew, 158
Holmes, Oliver Wendell, 127
Holmes, Sherlock, 116
Hope, Bob, 90
Hostile audience, 122, 221–235,
    248–249
    businesslike manner, 225–226
    closing, 233–235
    emotion, 232–233
    industry breakdown, 248
    pitfalls, 224–225
    postproblem bonding, 233–234
    presentation, 225–227, 227–235
    prove yourself, 230–232
    room setup, 226–227
    source of anger, 228–229
    take the high ground, 231–232

transitional moment, 232
venting, 227, 229–230
Humor. *See also* Humorous presentation
    competitive presentation, 215
    how often used, 255
    spontaneous, 85
Humorous presentation, 83–98
    adapt/localize humor, 90
    anger/hostility, 95
    closing, 96–98
    criticism, 96
    find material, 89
    joke, 86, 87
    key benefit, 95 96
    pitfalls, 85–87
    point of change, 87–89
    preparation, 87–94
    presentation, 94–98
    savers, 91–92
    "set up and punch" visuals, 93–94
    sharpen the humor, 90–91
    spontaneous humor, 85
Hyatt Corporation, 18

"I Have a Dream" (King), 70, 80–81
Iacocca, Lee, 13–14, 60, 120–121, 131,
    193–194, 228–229
Iacocca effect, 13–14
IBM, 172–173
Idea amnesty, 63
Idea origination story, 62
Imaginative presenters, 247
Immerse yourself, 106–107
Industry comparisons, 245–248
Information chameleon, 106–107
Inspirational presentation, 119–135
    build a congregation, 130–131
    closing, 135
    connect to bigger picture, 126–127
    doubt, 131
    examples, 132
    help people, 128

hostile audience, 122
    pitfalls, 122–123
    preparation, 123–128
    presentation, 129–135
    small, everyday events, 124–125
    step back, 125–126
    target a competitor, 117–118
    understandability, 132–134
    vision, 123, 126
Instructive incidents, 39–40
iPod, 204–205
iPod Shuffle, 205
"It's my fault," 150–151

Jackson, Mahalia, 81
James, William, 17
Jobs, Steven, 22–23, 26, 125, 135,
    204–205
Johnson, Ron, 160
Joke, 86, 87
Joke book, 89
June bug, 145–146

Kawasaki, Guy, 128
Kennedy, John F., 70, 132–134,
    222–223, 231, 255, 257
Kennedy, Robert, 222
Kettering, Charles, 171
Khrushchev, Nikita, 134
Kickers (surprises), 22–24
Kindall, Gary, 173
King, Martin Luther, Jr., 19–20, 70,
    80–81, 124, 125, 255, 257

Landmines, 100–102, 161–162
Language, 164–165
Laying out the facts, 99–117
    closing, 116–117
    clues to audience decision-making
        process, 115–116
    dramatize key facts, 111–113
    emotional logic card, 114

immerse yourself, 106–107
    information chameleon, 106–107
    logical structure, 107–108
    pitfalls, 102–104
    preparation, 104–113
    presentation, 114–117
    proof, 102–104
    surprise fact, 113
Leadership (Guiliani), 78
Leeds, Douglas B., 178
Lescher, Richard, 124
Likeability, 74
Lincoln, Abraham, 72, 95, 99
Lipp, Bob, 109, 128
Logical structure, 107–108
Longfellow, Henry Wadsworth, 28

Magic mentalism, 10
Magic track, 10–11
Mandela, Nelson, 138–139
Manufacturing industry, 245–248
Marketing budget, 197
May, Pete, 23
McGrane, Myles, 210
Medical services industry, 245–248
Melton, Joanne, vii,
Mental ladder, 207–208
Microsoft, 172–173
Moments of trust, 159–163
"Money Song, The," 6
Money timeline, 200–211
Morgan, Bob, 97
Morita, Akio, 186
Motivational greed, 194
MS-DOS, 173
Murdoch, Rupert, 1

Negative reactions, 218
Negative selling, 216
New idea, 53–67
    abstract thinking, 56
    adapt the idea/give it away, 66–67

attention grab, 61–62
audience focus, 59–60
baby steps, 63–64
closing, 65–67
concerns/objections, 65
distorting the idea, 56
idea amnesty, 63
implementation, 65–66
own the idea, 57
pitfalls, 35–36
preparation, 58–61
presentation, 61–67
proof, 64
risk aversion (audience), 60–61
selling the idea, 57–58
Newspaper articles, 110
Nixon, Richard, 144–145, 223
Nobel Peace Prize award ceremony
(1997), 76
Noble, Rick, 120
North American Van Lines, 93
Numbers/statistics, 241–257
building trust, 250–251, 254, 257
competitive presenters, 247
funniest presenters, 246
gender comparisons, 253–256
hostile audience, 248–249
humor, 255
imaginative presenters, 247
industry comparisons, 245–248
most pervasive strategies, 243–246,
254, 256, 257
most used strategies, 242
opening, 249–250
persuasive presenters, 255, 257
political party affiliation, 256–257
stories, 256

Objections, 65
Objectivity, 161
O'Brien, Ted, 9
Odyssey: Pepsi to Apple (Sculley), 135

Offering a solution, 171–184
assumptions, 177–178
build sequence, 182–183
closing, 183–184
context, 175, 176, 183
initial presentation, 178–183
look for "problem" to solve, 176–177
one obvious solution, 178
pitfalls, 174–175
preparation, 175–182
present several solutions in summary
form, 181
several solutions, 178–179
situation/context, 176, 180–181
One Fish Two Fish Red Fish Blue Fish
(Seuss), 63
Open-ended question, 9, 59
Opening, 240, 249–250
Opinion polls, 110. *See also*
Numbers/statistics
Origination story, 62
Overcoming hostility. *See* Hostile audience
Own the idea, 57

Pace
impact, 24–26
levels of sophistication, 12–13
Parks, Rosa, 124, 125
Passive voice, 239
Pauling, Linus, 53
Peale, Norman Vincent, 222
"Pepsi Challenge, The," 214–215
Perception. *See* Changing a perception
Perot, Ross, 156–157
Personal experience, 161–162
Persuasive presenters, 255, 257
Persuasiveness of strategies, 243–246,
254, 256, 257
Pieces of true cross, 239
PIS, 147
Political party affiliation, 256–257

Positioning the Battle for Your Mind
    (Ries/Trout), 207
Postproblem bonding, 233–234
Powell, Colin, 255, 257
Preacher King, The (Lescher), 124
Precision interface standard (PIS), 147
Presentation. *See also* individual subject
    headings
  audience involvement, 1–15
  changing a perception, 137–154
  competitive, 203–220
  creating excitement, 17–33
  emotional appeal, 69–82
  financial, 185–201
  hostile audience, 221–235
  humorous, 83–98
  inspirational, 119–135
  laying out facts, 99–117
  new idea, 53–67
  offering a solution, 171–184
  ranking, 241–257. *See also*
    Numbers/statistics
  telling a story, 35–51
  trust-building, 155–169
Presidential campaigns, 216
Price, Harrison "Buzz," 2
Pro-change statement, 150
Problem-solving, 7–8. *See also* Offering a
    solution
Professional services industry, 245–248
Proof
  fact-based presentations, 102–104,
    110–111
  new ideas, 64
  trust building, 162–163
  types of, 110–111
Proulx, Michel, 126, 175, 182–183
Prove yourself, 230–232
Proxmire, William, 228, 229

Radner, Gilda, 83
Ranking the strategies. *See* Numbers/
    statistics

Rayburn, Sam, 222
Reagan, Ronald, 13, 84, 255, 257
Reality, 161–162
Reck, George, 222
Redefine process of evaluation,
    144–145
Reinhardt, Jeff, 10
Relevancy, 5–6
Ries, Al, 207
Risk aversion (audience), 60–61
Robbins, Tony, 137
Rogers, Andy, 225–226
ROI presentation. *See* Financial
    presentation
Room setup, 11, 226–227

Rosenberg, Ann Belle, 213, 230–231
Rosenberg, David, 114, 116–117, 195,
    196
Rosenberg, David Frank, 28
Ross, David, 10, 126–127
Rowland, Helen, 185

Saint-Exupery, Antoine de, 119
Sams, Jack, 172–173
Sandbag, 240
Sandwich-grabbing frenzy, 143–144
Sarnoff, David, 203
Savers, 91–92
Scelba, David, 5, 6
Schickel, Richard, 2
Schiff, Herb, 208, 215
Schwanter, Gerhardt, 94, 167
Sculley, John, 22, 135, 214–215
Scutt, Der, 18
Seachange Technology, 57–58
Self-interest, 167–168
Sell sheets, 216
*Selling 2.0: Motivating Customers in the
    New Economy* (Gordon), 13, 210,
    270
SellingPower magazine, 77, 167, *253*
Selling the Dream (Kawasaki), 128

"Selling through a Slump" (Gordon), 109
"Set up and punch" visuals, 93–94
Side-by-side comparisons, 212, 219
Silber, Tony, 96
Singer, Tania, 163
Situation/context, 176, 180–181
Smart, 75
Smith, Adam, 185
Smith, Norwood, 24, 32
Solution. *See* Offering a solution
Sony Corporation, 186
Sophistication, 12–13
South Africa, 138–139
Spontaneity, 10
Spontaneous humor, 85
Spratling, Nigel, 95–96, 147
Sprung, Shelby, 120
Steinbeck, John, 35
Step back, 125–126
Stories, 239. *See also* Telling a story
    changing a perception, 147–148
    financial presentation, 195–197
    how often used, 256
    your own conversion, 62
Storyboard, 73–74
Strategies. *See* Presentation
Surprise fact, 113
Surprises (kickers), 22–24
Surveys, 110. *See also* Numbers/statistics
Swank, Hilary, 25
Szasz, Thomas, 137

Take the high ground, 231–232
Taylor, Elizabeth, 1
Taylor, Maurice "Morry," 54
Technical specs, 111
Telling a story, 35–51
    audience feedback, 49–50
    boil it down, 41
    closing, 50–51
    crisis point, 41–42
    dramatic structure, 48–49
    dull words, 43

exaggeration, 47
instructive incidents, 39–40
introduction, 47–48
main character, 41
photographs/pictures, 44
pitfalls, 38
preparation, 39–47
presentation, 47–51
sharpen the story, 44–47
three-act formula, 48–49
visual images, 43
Testimonials, 111
Testimony against interest, 239
That Perception Thing (Brown), 147
Thibeault, Evilee, 5–6
"Thinking person," 75
Thoreau, Henry David, 162
Thought leaders, 152
Three-act formula, 48–49
"Times They Are a-Changing, The"
    (Dylan), 22
Tokyo Tsushin Kogyo, 186
Torrey, John, 162
*Tough Calls: Selling Strategies to Win Over
    Your Most Difficult Customers*
    (Gordon), 12, 270
Tracy, Brian, 243
Trade advertising, 192
Transitional moment, 232
Trask, Dick, 227
Tremblay, Christian, 190, 195
Trewhitt, Henry, 84
Triola, Dennis, 190
Trout, Jack, 207
Trump, Donald, 18–19, 197
Trust-building presentation, 155–169
    anticipate trust level, 158–159
    audience risk, 158
    closing, 168–169
    dress (attire), 164
    entitlement devil, 167
    familiarity, 160
    first impression, 163–164

guarantee, 163
hot buttons, 165–167
language, 164–165
moments of trust, 159–163
objectivity, 161
personal experience, 161–162
pitfalls, 157–158
preparation, 158–163
presentation, 163–169
proof, 162–163
reality, 161–162
self-interest, 167–168
summary of reassurances, 169
surveys/opinion polls, 250–251,
   254, 257
understandability, 160–161
Trust hot buttons, 165–167
Trust Imperative, The (Dow et al.), 157
Truthfulness, 239
Tutu, Desmond, 76
Twain, Mark, 35, 85, 99, 155, 221

Understandability, 132–134, 160–161
"Using Questions to Close More Sales"
   (Gordon), 59

Value-shift moments, 220
Venting, 227, 229–230
Venture capital, 198
Vice president of finance, 199
Vision, 123, 126
Visualization, 32–33
Voice of America, 134

Wall, Ron, 48, 72
Walt Disney Company, 2–3, 198
Walters, Lilly, 91
Ward, William Arthur, 119
Wasp, 25
Watson, Thomas J., Sr., 155, 164
We Try Harder, 214
What-if scenarios, 62, 197
*What to Say When You're…Dying on the
   Platform* (Walters), 91
White, Jerry, 76, 101, 161
Wiesner, Pat, 8–9
Wilson, Woodrow, 137
Winston, Joel S., 163
Words ending in *-ing* and *-ion,* 240

Zaus, David, 33, 164

About the Author

Josh Gordon is president of Gordon Communication Strategies, a representation and training firm based in New York City. Gordon is a sought-after speaker and expert on the subject of sales and persuasion. He has been interviewed on CNN, CNBC, National Public Radio (on PRI's *Marketplace*), *The FORTUNE Business Report*, and Wall Street Journal TV.

Prior to beginning his sales career, Josh Gordon was an independent producer of training and informational programs. He produced programs for Polaroid Corporation, the American Management Associations, the U.S. Navy, the Social Security Administration, Litton Sweda International, and Data Terminal Systems.

In 1979, he attracted national attention while producing a series of 27 presentations for the U.S. Census Bureau that trained the 600,000 census workers who took the 1980 Decennial Census. It was the first time AV technology had been used for this function, and the first time it had been used on such a vast scale. The February 1980 issue of *Training* magazine, which interviewed Gordon, described the project as, "probably the largest civilian training program undertaken by anyone at anytime."

He is also the author of the best-selling books, *Tough Calls, Selling Strategies to Win over Your Most Difficult Customers* and *Selling 2.0, Motivating Customers in the New Economy* (both for sale online at Amazon.com).

These two books have been written up in *USA Today, FORTUNE, BusinessWeek, The Mail On Sunday* (UK), *Crain's New York Business, Selling Power,* and *Sales & Marketing Management.* The research findings from these two books have been the cover stories of over a dozen magazines and newsletters on the subject of selling and have been translated into German, Chinese, Korean, and Taiwanese.

He lives in Brooklyn, New York, with his wife, Lynn, and their two daughters.

Put the Persuasive Power of PRESENTATIONS THAT CHANGE MINDS to Work for Your Staff

Gordon Communication Strategies has developed a line of skills training programs, based on the principles of Josh Gordon's "Presentations That Change Minds," that can help your staff win more business.

Presentations are the heavy artillery of the persuasion process. While there are many tools of persuasion available to your staff, the face-to-face presentation is the venue reserved for convincing the most important customers, investors, and committees. Think how much more effective and profitable your organization would be if your staff could dramatically increase their persuasive power.

What makes our presentation training programs different is the emphasis on persuasive strategy. We do not talk about presenting to a generic, "one size fits all" audience. Every audience is unique and requires a different approach.

At the conclusion of training, your staff will know how to:

→ Research an audience before they get in front of them

→ Develop a persuasive strategy based on an audience's unique characteristics

→ Customize content, exercises, and visuals to create a persuasive event

→ Position your product or option against competitors

→ Deliver the informational performance of a lifetime

→ Deeply involve their audience

→ Develop a dialogue that goes "beyond the obvious"

→ Understand the serious business of using persuasive humor

→ Use the power of stories to persuade

→ Understand how to get commitment or change

And finally…

→ Your staff will develop a presentation that can be put to work the next business day.

It's real world. It's fun. It works.
We offer customized workshops and online training.
For more information visit our Web site:
www.JoshGordon.com
Or call us in New York City 718-802-0488
Ask for Lynn Gordon, Director of Training Services

What People are Saying About
Josh Gordon's Sales Training Workshops...

From Los Angeles to New York City, on the road and online, sales training designed by Josh Gordon can add excitement and persuasion power to your staff.

> *"With your combination of live exercises and visualized talks, you structured a presentation that gave all levels of our sales team a better understanding of how to sell in tough times. Our team found your training informative, entertaining, and valuable."*—Los Angeles Magazine

> *"I was amazed to read in their evaluations that they actually attributed sales success on individual accounts to one or more of your sessions... They voted you THE BEST in my three years selecting a trainer."*—Crain's New York Business

> *"...a real world presentation that got them thinking outside the box."*—North American Vanlines

> *"I am certain that our session together will have a positive and tangible impact on our business and our team attitude."*—PlanetOut Partners

> *"...fun, irreverent, and extremely effective. We enjoyed the fresh approaches you used to help us experience the lessons of sales persuasion, rather than just hear them in a presentation."*—MacDermid Printing Solutions

> *"My sales staff at Investment Advisor magazine is a street-smart and experienced group who is often skeptical of the sales trainers and coaching services we provide. You were a hit. My entire team agrees that you ran a great session."*—Investment Advisor

"...invigorated their thinking by providing a new way to address specific sales and customer issues, with practical ideas to use immediately."—Chyron Corporation

For more information visit our Web site at www.JoshGordon.com or call 718-802-0488